fastand
healthy

*Over 100 delicious good-for-you
recipes in no time at all*

flora airey

southwater

This edition is published by Southwater

Southwater is an imprint of Anness Publishing Ltd
Hermes House, 88–89 Blackfriars Road, London SE1 8HA
tel. 020 7401 2077; fax 020 7633 9499
www.southwaterbooks.com; info@anness.com

© Anness Publishing Ltd 1995, 2004

UK agent: The Manning Partnership Ltd,
6 The Old Dairy, Melcombe Road, Bath BA2 3LR;
tel. 01225 478444; fax 01225 478440; sales@manning-partnership.co.uk

UK distributor: Grantham Book Services Ltd,
Isaac Newton Way, Alma Park Industrial Estate, Grantham, Lincs NG31 9SD;
tel. 01476 541080; fax 01476 541061; orders@gbs.tbs-ltd.co.uk

North American agent/distributor: National Book Network,
4501 Forbes Boulevard, Suite 200, Lanham, MD 20706;
tel. 301 459 3366; fax 301 429 5746; www.nbnbooks.com

Australian agent/distributor: Pan Macmillan Australia,
Level 18, St Martins Tower, 31 Market St, Sydney, NSW 2000;
tel. 1300 135 113; fax 1300 135 103; customer.service@macmillan.com.au

New Zealand agent/distributor: David Bateman Ltd,
30 Tarndale Grove, Off Bush Road, Albany, Auckland;
tel. (09) 415 7664; fax (09) 415 8892

Publisher: Joanna Lorenz
Series Editor: Lindsay Porter
Designer: Peter Laws
Photographers: James Duncan, Michelle Garrett and Edward Allright
Stylists: Madeleine Brehaut, Michelle Garrett and Hilary Guy

Previously published as: *Fast & Healthy Recipes*

CONTENTS

INTRODUCTION

In recent years, our diet has come under such scrutiny that we are often confused about what we should or should not eat. It's not surprising that the latest trends in healthy eating are greeted with a certain amount of scepticism. Moderation never seems to be an issue – when advised to reduce fat, this is often translated as cutting out *all* fats, which often leaves us feeling deprived, and more likely to over indulge on the next occasion.

The recipes in this book do not claim to be able to help you lose weight, but neither will they leave you feeling disatisfied, or with cravings for 'forbidden' foods. They are based on the idea that plenty of fresh vegetables and grains, and small amounts of mono-unsaturated fats such as olive oil and that found in oily fish can be combined to provide nutritious meals that are undeniably delicious. Main courses, whether meat based or vegetarian, are hearty and satisfying, and there is a whole range of starters, light meals and accompaniments that can be made quickly, adding an interesting note to any meal. Indulgent desserts and baked treats have not been left out, so you can allow yourself to be tempted, safe in the knowledge that these foods are naturally good for you.

Devilled Onions en Croûte

Fill crisp bread cups with tender button onions tossed in a mustardy glaze.

Serves 4–6

INGREDIENTS
12 thin slices of white bread
225 g/8 oz baby button onions or
   shallots
150 ml/¼ pint/⅔ cup vegetable stock
15 ml/1 tbsp dry white wine or dry
   sherry
2 turkey rashers, cut into thin strips
10 ml/2 tsp Worcestershire sauce
5 ml/1 tsp tomato purée
¼ tsp prepared English mustard
salt and freshly ground black pepper
sprigs of flat-leaf parsley, to garnish

button onions

stock

white bread

parsley

turkey rashers

1 Pre-heat the oven to 200°C/400°F/ Gas 6. Stamp out the bread into rounds with a 7.5cm/3in fluted biscuit cutter and use to line a twelve-cup patty tin.

2 Cover each bread case with non-stick baking paper, and fill with baking beans or rice. Bake 'blind' for 5 minutes in the pre-heated oven. Remove the paper and beans and continue to bake for a further 5 minutes, until lightly browned and crisp.

3 Meanwhile, put the button onions in a bowl and cover with boiling water. Leave for 3 minutes, then drain and rinse under cold water. Trim off their top and root ends and slip them out of their skins.

4 Simmer the onions and stock in a covered saucepan for 5 minutes. Uncover and cook, stirring occasionally until the stock has reduced entirely. Add all the remaining ingredients, except the flat-leaf parsley. Cook for 2-3 minutes. Fill the toast cups with the devilled onions. Serve hot, garnished with sprigs of flat-leaf parsley.

Mini Pizzas

For a quick supper dish try these delicious little pizzas made with fresh and sun-dried tomatoes.

Makes 4

INGREDIENTS
1 × 150 g/5 oz packet pizza mix
8 halves sun-dried tomatoes in olive oil, drained
50 g/2 oz/½ cup black olives, stoned
225 g/8 oz ripe tomatoes, sliced
50 g/2 oz/¼ cup goat's cheese
30 ml/2 tbsp fresh basil leaves

basil

tomatoes

sun-dried tomatoes

black olives

goat's cheese

1 Preheat the oven to 200°C/400°F/ Gas 6. Make up the pizza base following the instructions on the side of the packet.

2 Divide the dough into 4 and roll each piece out to a 13 cm/5 in disc. Place on a lightly oiled baking sheet.

3 Place the sun-dried tomatoes and olives in a blender or food processor and blend until smooth. Spread the mixture evenly over the pizza bases.

4 Top with the tomato slices and crumble over the goat's cheese. Bake for 10–15 minutes. Sprinkle with the fresh basil and serve.

COOK'S TIP

You could use loose sun-dried tomatoes (preserved without oil) instead. Leave in a bowl of warm water for 10–15 minutes to soften, drain and blend with the olives.

Crunchy Baked Mushrooms with Dill Dip

These crispy-coated bites are ideal as an informal starter or served with drinks.

Serves 4–6

INGREDIENTS
115 g/4 oz/2 cups fresh fine white
    breadcrumbs
15 g/½ oz/1½ tbsp finely grated
    mature Cheddar cheese
5 ml/1 tsp paprika
225 g/8 oz button mushrooms
2 egg whites

FOR THE TOMATO AND DILL DIP
4 ripe tomatoes
115 g/4 oz/½ cup curd cheese
60 ml/4 tbsp natural low fat yogurt
1 garlic clove, crushed
30 ml/2 tbsp chopped fresh dill
salt and freshly ground black pepper
sprig of fresh dill, to garnish

paprika

mushrooms

dill

tomatoes

breadcrumbs

curd cheese

1 Pre-heat the oven to 190°C/375°F/Gas 5. Mix together the breadcrumbs, cheese and paprika in a bowl.

2 Wipe the mushrooms clean and trim the stalks, if necessary. Lightly whisk the egg whites with a fork, until frothy.

3 Dip each mushroom into the egg whites, then into the breadcrumb mixture. Repeat until all the mushrooms are coated.

4 Put the mushrooms on a non-stick baking sheet. Bake in the pre-heated oven for 15 minutes, or until tender and the coating has turned golden and crunchy.

5 Meanwhile, to make the dip, plunge the tomatoes into a saucepan of boiling water for 1 minute, then into a saucepan of cold water. Slip off the skins. Halve, remove the seeds and cores and roughly chop the flesh.

6 Put the curd cheese, yogurt, garlic clove and dill into a mixing bowl and combine well. Season to taste. Stir in the chopped tomatoes. Spoon the mixture into a serving dish and garnish with a sprig of fresh dill. Serve the mushrooms hot, together with the dip.

Buckwheat Blinis

These delectable light pancakes originated in Russia. For a special occasion, serve with a small glass of chilled vodka.

Serves 4

INGREDIENTS
5 ml/1 tsp easy-blend dry yeast
250 ml/8 fl oz/1 cup skimmed milk,
   warmed
40 g/1½ oz/⅓ cup buckwheat flour
40 g/1½ oz/⅓ cup plain flour
10ml/2 tsp caster sugar
pinch of salt
1 × size 3 egg, separated
oil, for frying

FOR THE AVOCADO CREAM
1 large avocado
75 g/3 oz/⅓ cup low fat fromage
   blanc
juice of 1 lime

FOR THE PICKLED BEETROOT
225 g/8 oz beetroot
45 ml/3 tbsp lime juice
snipped chives, to garnish
cracked black peppercorns, to garnish

beetroot

egg   avocado

buckwheat flour

lime   chives

fromage
blanc

skimmed milk

1 Mix the dry yeast with the milk, then mix with the next 4 ingredients and the egg yolk. Cover with a cloth and leave to prove for about 40 minutes. Whisk the egg white until stiff but not dry and fold into the blini mixture.

2 Heat a little oil in a non-stick pan and add a ladleful of batter to make a 10 cm/ 4 in pancake. Cook for 2–3 minutes on each side. Repeat with the remaining batter mixture to make 8 blinis.

3 Cut the avocado in half and remove the stone. Peel and place the flesh in a blender with the fromage blanc and lime juice. Blend until smooth.

4 Peel the beetroot and shred finely. Mix with the lime juice. To serve, top each blini with a spoonful of avocado cream. Serve with the pickled beetroot and garnish with snipped chives and cracked black peppercorns.

Soufflé Omelette

This delectable soufflé omelette is light and delicate enough to melt in the mouth.

Serves 1

INGREDIENTS
2 eggs, separated
30 ml/2 tbsp cold water
15 ml/1 tbsp chopped fresh coriander
salt and freshly ground black pepper
7.5 ml/½ tbsp olive oil
30 ml/2 tbsp mango chutney
25 g/1 oz/¼ cup Jarlsberg cheese, grated

Jarlsberg

mango chutney

eggs

coriander

COOK'S TIP

A light hand is essential to the success of this dish. Do not overmix the egg whites into the yolks or the mixture will be heavy.

1 Beat the egg yolks together with the cold water, coriander and seasoning.

2 Whisk the egg whites until stiff but not dry and gently fold into the egg yolk mixture.

3 Heat the oil in a frying pan, pour in the egg mixture and reduce the heat. Do not stir. Cook until the omelette becomes puffy and golden brown on the underside (carefully lift one edge with a palette knife to check).

4 Spoon on the chutney and sprinkle on the Jarlsberg. Fold over and slide onto a warm plate. Eat immediately. (If preferred, before adding the chutney and cheese, place the pan under a hot grill to set the top.)

Aubergine, Roast Garlic and Red Pepper Pâté

This is a simple pâté of smoky baked aubergine, sweet pink peppercorns and red peppers, with more than a hint of garlic!

Serves 4

INGREDIENTS
3 medium aubergines
2 red peppers
5 whole garlic cloves
7.5 ml/1½ tsp pink peppercorns in brine, drained and crushed
30 ml/2 tbsp chopped fresh coriander

aubergine

garlic

coriander

pink peppercorns

red pepper

1 Preheat the oven to 200°C/400°F/ Gas 6. Arrange the whole aubergines, peppers and garlic cloves on a baking sheet and place in the oven. After 10 minutes remove the garlic cloves and turn over the aubergines and peppers.

2 Peel the garlic cloves and place in the bowl of a blender.

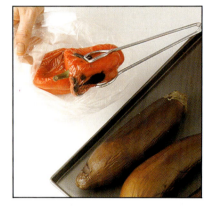

3 After a further 20 minutes remove the blistered and charred peppers from the oven and place in a plastic bag. Leave to cool.

4 After a further 10 minutes remove the aubergines from the oven. Split in half and scoop the flesh into a sieve placed over a bowl. Press the flesh with a spoon to remove the bitter juices.

5 Add the mixture to the garlic in the blender and blend until smooth. Place in a large mixing bowl.

6 Peel and chop the red peppers and stir into the aubergine mixture. Mix in the peppercorns and fresh coriander and serve at once.

Cheese and Onion Slice

This inexpensive supper dish is made substantial with the addition of porridge oats.

Serves 4

INGREDIENTS

2 large onions, thinly sliced
1 garlic clove, crushed
150 ml/¼ pint/⅔ cup vegetable stock
5 ml/1 tsp vegetable extract
250 g/9 oz/3 cups porridge oats
115 g/4 oz/1 cup grated Edam cheese
30 ml/2 tbsp chopped fresh parsley
2 eggs, lightly beaten
1 medium potato, peeled
salt and freshly ground black pepper
coleslaw and tomatoes, halved,
  to serve

porridge oats

Edam cheese

eggs

parsley

onion

potato

1 Pre-heat the oven to 180°C/350°F/Gas 4. Line the base of a 20 cm/8 in sandwich tin with non-stick baking paper. Put the onions, garlic clove and stock into a heavy-based saucepan and simmer until the stock has reduced entirely. Stir in the vegetable extract.

2 Spread the oats on a baking sheet and toast in the oven for 10 minutes. Mix with the onions, cheese, parsley, eggs, salt and freshly ground black pepper.

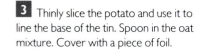

3 Thinly slice the potato and use it to line the base of the tin. Spoon in the oat mixture. Cover with a piece of foil.

4 Bake in the pre-heated oven for 35 minutes. Turn out onto a baking sheet and remove the lining paper. Put under a pre-heated hot grill to brown the potatoes. Cut into wedges and serve hot with coleslaw and halved tomatoes.

Potato Gratin

Don't rinse the potato slices before layering because the starch makes a thick sauce during cooking.

Serves 4

INGREDIENTS
1 garlic clove
5 large baking potatoes, peeled
45 ml/3 tbsp freshly grated Parmesan
  cheese
600 ml/1 pint/2½ cups vegetable or
  chicken stock
pinch of freshly grated nutmeg
salt and freshly ground black pepper

potatoes

Parmesan cheese

stock

1 Pre-heat the oven to 200°C/400°F/ Gas 6. Halve the garlic clove and rub over the base and sides of a gratin dish measuring about 20 × 30 cm/8 × 12 in.

2 Slice the potatoes very thinly and arrange a third of them in the dish. Sprinkle with a little grated cheese, salt and freshly ground black pepper. Pour over some of the stock to prevent the potatoes from discolouring.

3 Continue layering the potatoes and cheese as before, then pour over the rest of the stock. Sprinkle with the grated nutmeg.

4 Bake in the oven for 1¼-1½ hours or until the potatoes are tender and the tops well browned.

VARIATION

For a potato and onion gratin, thinly slice one medium onion and layer with the potato.

Cucumber and Alfalfa Tortillas

Wheat tortillas are extremely simple to prepare at home. Served with a crisp, fresh salsa, they make a marvellous light lunch or supper dish.

Serves 4

INGREDIENTS
225 g/8 oz/2 cups plain flour
pinch of salt
45 ml/3 tbsp olive oil
100 ml–150 ml/4–5 fl oz/½–⅔ cup
  warm water
lime wedges, to garnish

FOR THE SALSA
1 red onion, finely chopped
1 fresh red chilli, seeded and finely
  chopped
30 ml/2 tbsp chopped fresh dill or
  coriander
½ cucumber, peeled and chopped
175 g/6 oz alfalfa sprouts

FOR THE SAUCE
1 large avocado, peeled and stoned
juice of 1 lime
25 g/1 oz/2 tbsp soft goat's cheese
pinch of paprika

avocado

goat's
cheese

red chilli

cucumber

dill

alfalfa sprouts

1 Mix all the salsa ingredients together in a bowl and set aside.

2 To make the sauce, place the avocado, lime juice and goat's cheese in a food processor or blender and blend until smooth. Place in a bowl and cover with clear film. Dust with paprika just before serving.

COOK'S TIP
When peeling the avocado be sure to scrape off the bright green flesh from immediately under the skin as this gives the sauce its vivid green colour.

3 To make the tortillas, place the flour and salt in a food processor, add the oil and blend. Gradually add the water (the amount will vary depending on the type of flour). Stop adding water when a stiff dough has formed. Turn out onto a floured board and knead until smooth. Cover with a damp cloth.

4 Divide the mixture into 8 pieces. Knead each piece for a couple of minutes and form into a ball. Flatten and roll out each ball to a 23 cm/9 in circle.

5 Heat an ungreased heavy-based pan. Cook 1 tortilla at a time for about 30 seconds on each side. Place the cooked tortillas in a clean tea-towel and repeat until you have 8 tortillas.

6 To serve, spread each tortilla with a spoonful of avocado sauce, top with salsa and roll up. Garnish with lime wedges.

Cheese-stuffed Pears

These pears, with their scrumptious creamy topping, make a sublime dish when served with a simple salad.

Serves 4

INGREDIENTS
50 g/2 oz/¼ cup ricotta cheese
50 g/2 oz/¼ cup dolcelatte cheese
15 ml/1 tbsp honey
½ celery stick, finely sliced
8 green olives, stoned and roughly
  chopped
4 dates, stoned and cut into thin strips
pinch of paprika
4 ripe pears
150 ml/¼ pint/⅔ cup apple juice

honey

pear

apple juice

dates

dolcelatte

celery

olives

1 Preheat the oven to 200°C/400°F/ Gas 6. Place the ricotta in a bowl and crumble in the dolcelatte. Add the rest of the ingredients except for the pears and apple juice and mix well.

2 Halve the pears lengthwise and use a melon baller to remove the cores. Place in a ovenproof dish and divide the filling equally between them.

COOK'S TIP

Choose ripe pears in season such as Conference, William or Comice.

3 Pour in the apple juice and cover the dish with foil. Bake for 20 minutes or until the pears are tender.

4 Remove the foil and place the dish under a hot grill for 3 minutes. Serve immediately.

Nutty Chicken Balls

Serve these as a first course with the lemon sauce, or make into smaller balls and serve on cocktail sticks as canapés.

Serves 4

INGREDIENTS
355 g/12 oz chicken
50 g/2 oz/½ cup pistachio nuts, finely chopped
15 ml/1 tbsp lemon juice
2 eggs, beaten
plain flour, for shaping
75 g/3 oz/½ cup blanched chopped almonds
75 g/3 oz/¾ cup dried breadcrumbs
salt and freshly ground black pepper

FOR THE LEMON SAUCE
150 ml/¼ pint/⅔ cup chicken stock
225 g/8 oz/1¼ cups low fat cream cheese
15 ml/1 tbsp lemon juice
15 ml/1 tbsp chopped fresh parsley
15 ml/1 tbsp snipped fresh chives

chopped almonds   *minced chicken*

chives

pistachio nuts

breadcrumbs

lemon

parsley   *cream cheese*

1 Skin and mince or chop the chicken finely. Mix with salt and freshly ground black pepper, pistachio nuts, lemon juice, and one beaten egg.

2 Shape into sixteen small balls with floured hands (use a spoon as a guide, so that all the balls are roughly the same size). Roll the balls in the remaining beaten egg and coat with the almonds first and then the dried breadcrumbs, pressing on firmly. Chill until ready to cook.

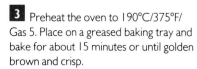

3 Preheat the oven to 190°C/375°F/Gas 5. Place on a greased baking tray and bake for about 15 minutes or until golden brown and crisp.

4 To make the lemon sauce, gently heat the chicken stock and cream cheese together in a pan, whisking until smooth. Add the lemon juice, herbs and season to taste. Serve with the chicken balls.

Bruschetta al Pomodoro

Bruschetta is an Italian garlic bread made with the best-quality olive oil you can find and pugliese, a coarse country bread, or ciabatta. Here, chopped tomatoes are added too.

Makes 2

INGREDIENTS
2 large thick slices coarse country
 bread
1 large garlic clove
60 ml/4 tbsp extra-virgin olive oil
2 ripe tomatoes, skinned and chopped
salt and pepper
1 sprig fresh basil, to garnish

country bread

tomatoes

garlic

1 Toast the bread on both sides.

2 Peel the garlic clove and squash with the flat side of a knife blade.

3 Rub the squashed garlic clove over the toast.

4 Drizzle half the olive oil over the toasted bread.

5 Top with the tomatoes, season well and drizzle over the remaining oil. Place under the grill to heat through, then garnish with sprig of basil and eat immediately.

PLAIN BRUSCHETTA
Rub a crushed garlic clove over untoasted bread, drizzle with oil and then toast.

Focaccia with Hot Artichokes and Olives

Focaccia makes an excellent base for different grilled toppings. Artichoke hearts bottled in oil are the best choice for this recipe.

Makes 3

INGREDIENTS
60 ml/4 tbsp olive paste
3 mini focaccia
1 small red pepper, halved and seeded
275 g/10 oz bottled or canned
    artichoke hearts, drained
75 g/3 oz pepperoni, sliced
5 ml/1 tsp dried oregano

red pepper

mini focaccia

oregano

pepperoni

artichoke hearts

1 Preheat the oven to 220°C/425°F/ Gas 7. Spread the olive paste over the focaccia. Grill the red pepper till blackened, put in a plastic bag, seal and allow to cool for 10 minutes. Skin the pepper and cut into strips.

2 Cut the artichoke hearts in quarters and arrange over the paste with the pepperoni.

3 Sprinkle over the red pepper strips and the oregano. Place in the oven for 5–10 minutes until heated through.

OLIVE FOCACCIA

Focaccia is an Italian flat bread made with olive oil and often with olives as well. The amount of water needed varies with the type of flour used, so you may need a little less – or a little more – than the given quantity.

Makes 2 loaves

450 g/1 lb/4 cups strong white flour
5 ml/1 tsp salt
5 ml/1 tsp dried yeast
300 ml/10 fl oz/1¼ cups warm water
pinch of sugar
60 ml/4 tbsp olive oil
100 g/4 oz/1 cup black olives, stoned
    and roughly chopped
2.5 ml/½ tsp dried oregano

Mix the flour and salt together in a mixing bowl. Put the yeast in a small bowl and mix with half the water and a pinch of sugar to help activate the yeast. Leave for about 10 minutes until dissolved. Add the yeast mixture to the flour along with the oil, olives and remaining water and mix to a soft

dough, adding a little more water if necessary.

Turn the dough out on to a floured surface and knead for 5 minutes until it is smooth and elastic. Place in a mixing bowl, cover with a damp tea towel and leave in a warm place to rise for about 2 hours or until doubled in size.

Preheat the oven to 220°C/425°F/ Gas 7. Turn the dough out on to a floured surface and knead again for a few minutes. Divide into 2 portions, then roll out each to a thickness of 1 cm/½ in in either a round or oblong shape. Place on an oiled baking sheet using a floured rolling pin to lift the dough. Make indentations all over the surface using your fingertips and sprinkle with the oregano. Bake in the oven for about 15–20 minutes.

FOCACCIA WITH MOZZARELLA AND SUN-DRIED TOMATOES

Spread the focaccia with 45 ml/3 tbsp chopped sun-dried tomatoes. Slice 225 g/8 oz mozzarella cheese and arrange over the top. Sprinkle with 8 stoned and quartered black olives, and heat through in the oven as for the main recipe.

MINI FOCACCIA

Divide the dough into 6 balls. On a floured surface roll these out to 15 cm/6 in circles. Finish as for Olive Focaccia, baking for 12–15 minutes.

Ham and Asparagus Slice

Be creative in your arrangement of the ingredients here. You could make ham cornets, or wrap the asparagus in the ham, or use different meats such as salami, mortadella or Black Forest ham.

Makes 4

INGREDIENTS
12 asparagus spears
100 g/4 oz/½ cup low fat cream
    cheese
4 slices rye bread
4 slices ham
few leaves curly endive
30 ml/2 tbsp mayonnaise
4 radish roses, to garnish

rye bread

curly endive

ham

asparagus

1 Cook the asparagus until tender, drain, pat dry with kitchen paper and cool.

2 Spread cream cheese over the rye bread and arrange the ham in folds over the top.

3 Lay 3 asparagus spears on each sandwich.

4 Arrange curly endive on top of the spears and spoon over some mayonnaise.

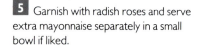

5 Garnish with radish roses and serve extra mayonnaise separately in a small bowl if liked.

SALAMI AND COTTAGE CHEESE SLICE

Omit the asparagus. Arrange 3 salami slices on top with a spoonful of cottage cheese and chopped fresh chives. Garnish with watercress, chives and chive flowers.

English Muffins with Sole, Spinach and Mushrooms

English muffins, frozen spinach and a few mushrooms form the beginning of this nourishing fish course. Any flatfish will do, although sole works best of all.

Serves 2

INGREDIENTS

115 g/4 oz/½ cup low fat spread
1 medium onion, chopped
115 g/4 oz brown button mushrooms, sliced
2 fresh thyme sprigs, chopped
275 g/10 oz frozen leaf spinach, thawed
1.5 kg/3 lb sole or plaice to yield 675 g/1½ lb skinned fillet
2 white English muffins, split
60 ml/4 tbsp low fat crème fraîche
salt and freshly ground black pepper

1 Heat 50 g/2 oz/4 tbsp of the low fat spread in a saucepan and add the onion. Cook over a gentle heat until soft but not coloured.

2 Add the mushrooms and thyme, cover and cook for a further 2–3 minutes. Remove the lid and increase the heat to drive off excess moisture.

English muffins

crème fraîche

spinach

sole

thyme

onion

3 Using the back of a large spoon, press the thawed frozen spinach in a sieve to extract the moisture.

4 Heat a further 25 g/1 oz/2 tbsp low fat spread in a saucepan, add the spinach, heat through and season to taste.

5 Melt the remaining low fat spread in a large frying pan, season the fillets and, with skin side uppermost, cook for 4 minutes, turning once.

COOK'S TIP

Approximately half of the weight of flatfish is bone, so if buying your fish whole, ask the fishmonger to give you the correct weight of boned fish.

6 Toast the muffins. Divide the fillets between them, top with spinach and a layer of mushrooms, then finish with a spoonful of crème fraîche.

Roquefort and Pear

Roquefort is delicious served with pear, but other blue cheeses such as Stilton or Cambozola can be used instead. Toasted brioche makes a good base but must be eaten straight away as it quickly becomes soft once filled.

Makes 4

INGREDIENTS
4 slices brioche loaf
125 g/4 oz/½ cup curd cheese
few sprigs rocket
125 g/4 oz Roquefort cheese, sliced
1 ripe pear, quartered, cored and
   sliced
juice of ½ lemon
4 pecan nuts, to garnish
viola flowers, to garnish (optional)

curd cheese

pears

rocket

pecan nuts

Roquefort cheese

1 Toast the brioche and spread with the curd cheese.

2 Arrange rocket leaves on top of the cheese.

3 Place the sliced Roquefort on top.

4 Brush the pear slices with lemon juice to prevent discoloration.

5 Arrange the pear slices, overlapping, in a fan shape on the cheese.

6 Garnish with pecan nuts (whole or chopped) and a viola flower if you wish.

Guacamole with Crudités

This fresh-tasting spicy dip is made using peas instead of the traditional avocados.

Serves 4–6

INGREDIENTS
350 g/12 oz/2¼ cups frozen peas, defrosted
1 garlic clove, crushed
2 spring onions, trimmed and chopped
5 ml/1 tsp finely grated rind and juice of 1 lime
2.5 ml/½ tsp ground cumin
dash of Tabasco sauce
15 ml/1 tbsp reduced calorie mayonnaise
30 ml/2 tbsp chopped fresh coriander
salt and freshly ground black pepper
pinch of paprika and lime slices, to garnish

FOR THE CRUDITÉS
6 baby carrots
2 celery sticks
1 red-skinned eating apple
1 pear
15 ml/1 tbsp lemon or lime juice
6 baby sweetcorn

peas

vegetables

1 Put the peas, garlic clove, spring onions, lime rind and juice, cumin, Tabasco sauce, mayonnaise and salt and freshly ground black pepper into a food processor or a blender for a few minutes and process until smooth.

2 Add the chopped coriander and process for a few more seconds. Spoon into a serving bowl, cover with clear film and chill in the refrigerator for 30 minutes, to let the flavours develop.

3 For the crudités, trim and peel the carrots. Halve the celery sticks lengthways and trim into sticks, the same length as the carrots. Quarter, core and thickly slice the apple and pear, then dip into the lemon or lime juice. Arrange with the baby sweetcorn on a platter.

4 Sprinkle the paprika over the guacamole and garnish with lime slices.

Minted Melon and Grapefruit Cocktail

Melon is always a popular starter. Here the flavour is complemented by the refreshing taste of citrus fruit and a simple dressing.

Serves 4

INGREDIENTS
1 small Galia melon, weighing about
  1 kg/2¼ lb
2 pink grapefruits
1 yellow grapefruit
5 ml/1 tsp Dijon mustard
5 ml/1 tsp raspberry or sherry vinegar
5 ml/1 tsp clear honey
15 ml/1 tbsp chopped fresh mint
sprigs of fresh mint, to garnish

grapefruits   mint

mustard   honey

vinegar

melon

1 Halve the melon and remove the seeds with a teaspoon. With a melon baller, carefully scoop the flesh into balls.

2 With a sharp knife, peel the grapefruit and remove all the white pith. Remove the segments by cutting between the membranes, holding the fruit over a small bowl to catch any juices.

3 Whisk the mustard, vinegar, honey, chopped mint and grapefruit juices together in a mixing bowl. Add the melon balls together with the grapefruit and mix well. Chill for 30 minutes.

4 Ladle into four dishes and serve garnished with a sprig of fresh mint.

Minestrone

A classic substantial winter soup originally from Milan, but found in various versions around the Mediterranean coasts of Italy and France. Cut the vegetables as roughly or as small as you like. Add freshly grated Parmesan cheese just before serving.

Serves 6–8

INGREDIENTS
225 g/8 oz/2 cups dried haricot
   beans
30 ml/2 tbsp olive oil
50 g/2 oz smoked streaky bacon,
   diced
2 large onions, sliced
2 garlic cloves, crushed
2 medium carrots, diced
3 celery sticks, sliced
400 g/14 oz canned chopped
   tomatoes
2.25 litres/4 pints/10 cups beef stock
350 g/12 oz potatoes, diced
175 g/6 oz/1½ cups small pasta
   shapes (macaroni, stars, shells, etc)
225 g/8 oz green cabbage, thinly
   sliced
175 g/6 oz fine green beans, sliced
100 g/4 oz/¾ cup frozen peas
45 ml/3 tbsp chopped fresh parsley
salt and pepper
freshly grated Parmesan cheese,
   to serve

celery

cabbage

carrots

pasta shapes

onions

bacon

garlic

green beans

1 Cover the beans with cold water and leave to soak overnight.

2 Heat the oil in a large saucepan and add the bacon, onions and garlic. Cover and cook gently for 5 minutes, stirring occasionally, until soft.

3 Add the carrots and celery and cook for 2–3 minutes until softening.

4 Drain the beans and add to the pan with the tomatoes and stock. Cover and simmer for 2–2½ hours, until the beans are tender.

5 Add the potatoes 30 minutes before the soup is finished.

VARIATION

To make Soupe au Pistou from the South of France, stir in a basil, garlic and pine nut sauce (pesto or pistou) just before serving.

6 Add the pasta, cabbage, beans, peas and parsley 15 minutes before the soup is ready. Season to taste and serve with a bowl of freshly grated Parmesan cheese.

Red Onion and Beetroot Soup

This beautiful vivid ruby-red soup will look stunning at any dinner party.

Serves 4–6

INGREDIENTS
15 ml/1 tbsp olive oil
350 g/12 oz red onions, sliced
2 garlic cloves, crushed
275 g/10 oz cooked beetroot, cut into
  sticks
1.1 litres/2 pints/5 cups vegetable
  stock or water
50 g/2 oz/1 cup cooked soup pasta
30 ml/2 tbsp raspberry vinegar
salt and freshly ground black pepper
low fat yogurt or fromage blanc, to
  garnish
snipped chives, to garnish

garlic

red onion

beetroot

pasta

chives

1 Heat the olive oil and add the onions and garlic.

2 Cook gently for about 20 minutes or until soft and tender.

COOK'S TIP
Try substituting cooked barley for the pasta to give extra nuttiness.

3 Add the beetroot, stock or water, cooked pasta shapes and vinegar and heat through. Season to taste.

4 Ladle into bowls. Top each one with a spoonful of yogurt or fromage blanc and sprinkle with chives.

Cauliflower, Flageolet and Fennel Seed Soup

The sweet, anise-liquorice flavour of the fennel seeds gives a delicious edge to this hearty soup.

Serves 4–6

INGREDIENTS
15 ml/1 tbsp olive oil
1 garlic clove, crushed
1 onion, chopped
10 ml/2 tsp fennel seeds
1 cauliflower, cut into small florets
2 × 400 g/14 oz cans flageolet beans,
    drained and rinsed
1.1 litres/2 pints/5 cups vegetable
    stock or water
salt and freshly ground black pepper
chopped fresh parsley, to garnish
toasted slices of French bread, to
    serve

flageolet beans

French bread

onion

garlic

cauliflower

fennel seeds

parsley

1 Heat the olive oil. Add the garlic, onion and fennel seeds and cook gently for 5 minutes or until softened.

2 Add the cauliflower, half of the beans and the stock or water.

3 Bring to the boil. Reduce the heat and simmer for 10 minutes or until the cauliflower is tender.

4 Pour the soup into a blender and blend until smooth. Stir in the remaining beans and season to taste. Reheat and pour into bowls. Sprinkle with chopped parsley and serve with toasted slices of French bread.

Italian Bean and Pasta Soup

A thick and hearty soup which, followed by bread and cheese, makes a substantial lunch.

Serves 6

INGREDIENTS

175 g/6 oz/1½ cups dried haricot
  beans, soaked overnight in
  cold water
1.75 litres/3 pints/7½ cups chicken
  stock or water
100 g/4 oz/1 cup medium pasta shells
60 ml/4 tbsp olive oil, plus extra to
  serve
2 garlic cloves, crushed
60 ml/4 tbsp chopped fresh parsley
salt and pepper

parsley

haricot beans

pasta shells

garlic

1 Drain the beans and place in a large saucepan with the stock or water. Simmer, half-covered, for 2–2½ hours or until tender.

2 Liquidize half the beans and a little of their cooking liquid, then stir into the remaining beans in the pan.

3 Add the pasta and simmer gently for 15 minutes until tender. (Add extra water or stock if the soup seems too thick.)

4 Heat the oil in a small pan and fry the garlic until golden. Stir into the soup with the parsley and season well with salt and pepper. Ladle into individual bowls and drizzle each with a little extra olive oil.

Italian Vegetable Soup

The success of this clear soup depends on the quality of the stock, so use home-made vegetable stock rather than stock cubes.

Serves 4

INGREDIENTS

1 small carrot
1 baby leek
1 celery stick
50 g/2 oz green cabbage
900 ml/1½ pints/3¾ cups
    vegetable stock
1 bay leaf
115 g/4 oz/1 cup cooked cannellini
    beans
25 g/1 oz/⅕ cup soup pasta, such as
    tiny shells, bows, stars or elbows
salt and freshly ground black pepper
snipped fresh chives, to garnish

stock

cabbage

bay leaf

chives

baby leek

celery

carrot

pasta

1 Cut the carrot, leek and celery into 5 cm/2 in long julienne strips. Slice the cabbage very finely.

2 Put the stock and bay leaf into a large saucepan and bring to the boil. Add the carrot, leek and celery, cover and simmer for 6 minutes.

3 Add the cabbage, beans and pasta shapes. Stir, then simmer uncovered for a further 4-5 minutes, or until the vegetables and pasta are tender.

4 Remove the bay leaf and season to taste. Ladle into four soup bowls and garnish with snipped chives. Serve immediately.

Tabbouleh with Fennel and Pomegranate

A fresh salad originating in the Middle East, with the added crunchiness of fennel and sweet pomegranate seeds. It is perfect for a summer lunch.

Serves 6

INGREDIENTS
225 g/8 oz/1 cup bulgur wheat
2 fennel bulbs
1 small fresh red chilli, seeded and
    finely chopped
1 celery stick, finely sliced
30 ml/2 tbsp olive oil
finely grated rind and juice of 2
    lemons
6–8 spring onions, chopped
90 ml/6 tbsp chopped fresh mint
90 ml/6 tbsp chopped fresh parsley
1 pomegranate, seeds removed
salt and freshly ground black pepper

lemon

red chilli

celery

bulgur wheat

spring onion

fennel

pomegranate

parsley

mint

I Place the bulgur wheat in a bowl and pour over enough cold water to cover. Leave to stand for 30 minutes.

2 Drain the wheat through a sieve, pressing out any excess water using a spoon.

3 Halve the fennel bulbs and cut into very fine slices.

4 Mix all the remaining ingredients together, including the soaked bulgur wheat and fennel. Season well, cover, and set aside for 30 minutes before serving.

Buckwheat Couscous with Goat's Cheese and Celery

Couscous is made from cracked, partially cooked wheat, which is dried and then reconstituted in water or stock. It tastes of very little by itself, but carries the flavour of other ingredients very well.

Serves 4

INGREDIENTS
1 egg
30 ml/2 tbsp olive oil
1 small bunch spring onions, chopped
2 celery sticks, sliced
175 g/6 oz/1 cup couscous
75 g/3 oz/½ cup buckwheat
45 ml/3 tbsp chopped fresh parsley
finely grated zest of ½ lemon
25 g/1 oz/¼ cup chopped walnuts, toasted
150 g/5 oz strongly flavoured goat's cheese
salt and freshly ground black pepper
Cos lettuce leaves, to serve

buckwheat

celery

egg

goat's cheese

parsley

walnuts

1 Boil the egg for 10 minutes, cool, peel and set aside. Heat the oil in a saucepan and add the spring onions and celery. Cook for 2–3 minutes until soft.

2 Add the couscous and buckwheat and cover with 600 ml/1 pint/2½ cups of boiling salted water. Cover and return to a simmer. Remove from the heat and allow the couscous to soften and absorb the water for about 3 minutes. Transfer the mixture to a large bowl.

3 Grate the hard-boiled egg finely into a small bowl and add the chopped parsley, lemon zest and walnuts. Fold into the couscous, season, and crumble in the goat's cheese. Mix well and then turn out into a shallow dish. Serve warm with a salad of Cos lettuce.

VARIATION
Couscous is ideal as a filling for pitta breads when accompanied with crisp salad leaves.

Red Pepper Polenta with Sunflower Salsa

This recipe is inspired by Italian and Mexican cookery. Cornmeal polenta is a staple food in Italy, served with brightly coloured vegetables. Mexican *Pipian* is made from sunflower seeds, chilli and lime.

Serves 4

INGREDIENTS
3 young courgettes
oil, for greasing
1.2 litres/2 pints/5 cups light
   vegetable stock
250 g/9 oz/2 cups fine polenta or
   cornmeal
1 × 200 g/7 oz can red peppers,
   drained and sliced
115 g/4 oz green salad, to serve

FOR THE SUNFLOWER SALSA
75 g/3 oz sunflower seeds, toasted
50 g/2 oz/1 cup crustless
   white bread
200 ml/7 fl oz/scant 1 cup
   vegetable stock
1 garlic clove, crushed
½ red chilli, seeded and chopped
30 ml/2 tbsp chopped fresh coriander
5 ml/1 tsp sugar
15 ml/1 tbsp lime juice
pinch of salt

1 Bring a saucepan of salted water to the boil. Add the courgettes and simmer over a low heat for 2–3 minutes. Refresh under cold running water and drain. When they are cool, cut into strips.

polenta

sunflower seeds

courgettes

limes

red chillies

red peppers

coriander

white bread

2 Lightly oil a 23 cm/9 in loaf tin and line with a single sheet of greaseproof paper.

3 Bring the vegetable stock to a simmer in a heavy saucepan. Add the polenta in a steady stream, stirring continuously for about 2–3 minutes until thickened.

4 Partly fill the lined tin with the polenta mixture. Layer the sliced courgettes and peppers over the polenta. Fill the tin with the remaining polenta and leave to set for about 10–15 minutes. Polenta should be served warm or at room temperature.

COOK'S TIP

Sunflower salsa will keep for up to 10 days in the refrigerator. It is delicious poured over a simple dish of pasta.

5 To make the salsa, grind the sunflower seeds to a thick paste in a food processor. Add the remaining ingredients and combine thoroughly.

6 Turn the warm polenta out onto a board, remove the paper and cut into thick slices with a large wet knife. Serve with the salsa and a green salad.

Chilli Bean Bake

The contrasting textures of saucy beans, vegetables and crunchy cornbread topping make this a memorable meal.

Serves 4

INGREDIENTS
225 g/8 oz/1⅓ cups red kidney beans
1 bay leaf
1 large onion, finely chopped
1 garlic clove, crushed
2 celery sticks, sliced
5 ml/1 tsp ground cumin
5 ml/1 tsp chilli powder
400 g/14 oz can chopped tomatoes
15 ml/1 tbsp tomato purée
5 ml/1 tsp dried mixed herbs
15 ml/1 tbsp lemon juice
1 yellow pepper, seeded and diced
salt and freshly ground black pepper
mixed salad, to serve

FOR THE CORNBREAD TOPPING
175 g/6 oz/1½ cups corn meal
15 ml/1 tbsp wholemeal flour
5 ml/1 tsp baking powder
1 egg, beaten
175 ml/6 fl oz/¾ cup skimmed milk

kidney beans

celery

tomato purée

pepper

1 Soak the beans overnight in cold water. Drain and rinse well. Pour 1 litre/ 1¾ pints/4 cups of water into a large, heavy-based saucepan together with the beans and bay leaf and boil rapidly for 10 minutes. Lower the heat, cover and simmer for 35–40 minutes, or until the beans are tender.

2 Add the onion, garlic clove, celery, cumin, chilli powder, chopped tomatoes, tomato purée and dried mixed herbs. Half-cover the pan with a lid and simmer for a further 10 minutes.

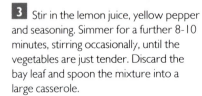

3 Stir in the lemon juice, yellow pepper and seasoning. Simmer for a further 8-10 minutes, stirring occasionally, until the vegetables are just tender. Discard the bay leaf and spoon the mixture into a large casserole.

4 Pre-heat the oven to 220°C/425°F/ Gas 7. For the topping, put the corn meal, flour, baking powder and a pinch of salt into a bowl and mix together. Make a well in the centre and add the egg and milk. Mix and pour over the bean mixture. Bake in the pre-heated oven for 20 minutes, or until brown.

Cannellini Bean Pureé with Grilled Radicchio

The slightly bitter flavours of the radicchio and chicory make a wonderful marriage with the creamy citrus bean purée.

Serves 4

INGREDIENTS

1 × 400 g/14 oz can cannellini beans
45 ml/3 tbsp low fat fromage blanc
finely grated zest, rind and juice of 1
　large orange
15 ml/1 tbsp finely chopped fresh
　rosemary
4 heads of chicory
2 medium radicchio
15 ml/1 tbsp walnut oil

chicory

fromage blanc

cannellini
beans

rosemary

raddichio

orange

1 Drain the beans, rinse, and drain again. Purée the beans in a blender or food processor with the fromage blanc, orange zest, orange juice and rosemary. Set aside.

2 Cut the chicory in half lengthwise.

3 Cut each radicchio into 8 wedges

4 Lay out the chicory and radicchio on a baking tray and brush with walnut oil. Grill for 2–3 minutes. Serve with the puree and scatter over the orange rind.

COOK'S TIP
Other suitable beans to use are haricot, mung or broad beans.

Pumpkin and Pistachio Risotto

This elegant combination of creamy golden rice and orange pumpkin can be as pale or bright as you like by adding different quantities of saffron.

Serves 4

INGREDIENTS
1.1 litres/2 pints/5 cups vegetable
   stock or water
generous pinch of saffron threads
30 ml/2 tbsp olive oil
1 medium onion, chopped
2 garlic cloves, crushed
450 g/1 lb arborio rice
900 g/2 lb pumpkin, peeled, seeded
   and cut into 2 cm/¾ in cubes
200 ml/7 fl oz/¾ cup dry white wine
15 g/½ oz Parmesan cheese, finely
   grated
50 g/2 oz/½ cup pistachios
45 ml/3 tbsp chopped fresh marjoram
   or oregano, plus extra leaves, to
   garnish
salt, freshly grated nutmeg and ground
   black pepper

saffron

pumpkin

white wine

onion

garlic

marjoram

Parmesan

arborio rice

pistachios

1 Bring the stock or water to the boil and reduce to a low simmer. Ladle a little stock into a small bowl. Add the saffron threads and leave to infuse.

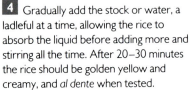

4 Gradually add the stock or water, a ladleful at a time, allowing the rice to absorb the liquid before adding more and stirring all the time. After 20–30 minutes the rice should be golden yellow and creamy, and *al dente* when tested.

2 Heat the oil in a large saucepan. Add the onion and garlic and cook gently for about 5 minutes until softened. Add the rice and pumpkin and cook for a few more minutes until the rice looks transparent.

3 Pour in the wine and allow it to bubble hard. When it is absorbed add ¼ of the stock and the infused saffron and liquid. Stir constantly until all the liquid is absorbed.

5 Stir in the Parmesan cheese, cover the pan and leave to stand for 5 minutes.

6 To finish, stir in the pistachios and marjoram or oregano. Season to taste with a little salt, nutmeg and pepper, and scatter over a few extra marjoram or oregano leaves.

COOK'S TIP
Italian arborio rice must be used to make an authentic risotto. Choose unpolished white arborio as it contains more starch.

Lemon and Ginger Spicy Beans

An extremely quick delicious meal, made with canned beans for speed. You probably won't need extra salt as canned beans tend to be already salted.

Serves 4

INGREDIENTS

5 cm/2 in piece fresh ginger root,
  peeled and roughly chopped
3 garlic cloves, roughly chopped
250 ml/8 fl oz/1 cup cold water
15 ml/1 tbsp sunflower oil
1 large onion, thinly sliced
1 fresh red chilli, seeded and finely
  chopped
¼ tsp cayenne pepper
10 ml/2 tsp ground cumin
5 ml/1 tsp ground coriander
½ tsp ground turmeric
30 ml/2 tbsp lemon juice
75 g/3 oz/⅓ cup chopped fresh
  coriander
1 × 400 g/14 oz can black-eyed beans,
  drained and rinsed
1 × 400 g/14 oz can aduki beans,
  drained and rinsed
1 × 400 g/14 oz can haricot beans,
  drained and rinsed
freshly ground black pepper

garlic
red chilli
ginger
ground coriander
ground turmeric
ground cumin
haricot beans
onion
aduki beans
black-eyed beans

1 Place the ginger, garlic and 60 ml/ 4 tbsp of the cold water in a blender and mix until smooth.

2 Heat the oil in a pan. Add the onion and chilli and cook gently for 5 minutes until softened.

3 Add the cayenne pepper, cumin, ground coriander and turmeric and stir-fry for 1 minute.

4 Stir in the ginger and garlic paste from the blender and cook for another minute.

5 Add the remaining water, lemon juice and fresh coriander, stir well and bring to the boil. Cover the pan tightly and cook for 5 minutes.

6 Add all the beans and cook for a further 5–10 minutes. Season with pepper and serve.

Vegetarian Cassoulet

Every town in south-west France has its own version of this popular classic. Warm French bread is all that is needed to complete this hearty vegetable version.

Serves 4–6

INGREDIENTS
400 g/14 oz/2 cups dried
   haricot beans
1 bay leaf
2 onions
3 whole cloves
2 garlic cloves, crushed
5 ml/1 tsp olive oil
2 leeks, thickly sliced
12 baby carrots
115 g/4 oz button mushrooms
400 g/14 oz can chopped tomatoes
15 ml/1 tbsp tomato purée
5 ml/1 tsp paprika
15 ml/1 tbsp chopped fresh thyme
30 ml/2 tbsp chopped fresh parsley
115 g/4 oz/2 cups fresh white
   breadcrumbs
salt and freshly ground black pepper

chopped tomatoes   *bay leaf*

leek

breadcrumbs

carrots

mushrooms

COOK'S TIP

If you're short of time use canned haricot beans – you'll need two 400 g/ 14 oz cans. Drain, reserving the bean juices and make up to 400 ml/14 fl oz/1⅔ cups with vegetable stock.

1 Soak the beans overnight in plenty of cold water. Drain and rinse under cold running water. Put them in a saucepan together with 1.75 litres/3 pints/7½ cups of cold water and the bay leaf. Bring to the boil and cook rapidly for 10 minutes.

2 Peel one of the onions and spike with cloves. Add to the beans and reduce the heat. Cover and simmer gently for 1 hour, until the beans are almost tender. Drain, reserving the stock but discarding the bay leaf and onion.

3 Chop the remaining onion and put it into a large flameproof casserole together with the garlic cloves and olive oil. Cook gently for 5 minutes, or until softened.

4 Pre-heat the oven to 170°C/325°F/ Gas 3. Add the leeks, carrots, mushrooms, chopped tomatoes, tomato purée, paprika, thyme and 400 ml/ 14 fl oz/1⅔ cups of the reserved stock to the casserole.

5 Bring to the boil, cover and simmer gently for 10 minutes. Stir in the cooked beans and parsley. Season to taste.

OK – ish

6 Sprinkle with the breadcrumbs and bake uncovered in the pre-heated oven for 35 minutes, or until the topping is golden brown and crisp.

Risotto-stuffed Aubergines with Spicy Tomato Sauce

Aubergines are a challenge to the creative cook and allow for some unusual recipe ideas. Here, they are stuffed and baked with a cheese and pine nut topping.

Serves 4

INGREDIENTS
4 small aubergines
105 ml/7 tbsp olive oil
1 small onion, chopped
175 g/6 oz/scant 1 cup arborio rice
750 ml/1¼ pints/3⅔ cups
   vegetable stock
15 ml/1 tbsp white wine vinegar
8 fresh basil sprigs, to garnish

FOR THE TOPPING
25 g/1 oz/¼ cup freshly grated
   Parmesan cheese
15 g/½ oz/1 tbsp pine nuts

FOR THE TOMATO SAUCE
300 ml/½ pint/1¼ cups thick passata
   or tomato pulp
5 ml/1 tsp mild curry paste
pinch of salt

aubergines

onion

pine nuts

*Parmesan
cheese*

passata

rice

COOK'S TIP

Don't be put off by the amount of oil aubergines absorb when cooking. Use olive oil and remember that good oils are low in saturated fat and are believed to fight against heart disease.

1 Preheat the oven to 200°C/400°F/Gas 6. Cut the aubergines in half lengthways and take out their flesh with a small knife. Brush with 30 ml/2 tbsp of the oil, place on a baking sheet and cook in the preheated oven for 6–8 minutes.

2 Chop the reserved aubergine flesh and heat the remainder of the olive oil in a medium saucepan. Add the aubergine flesh and the onion and cook over a gentle heat for 3–4 minutes until soft.

3 Add the rice, stir in the stock and simmer uncovered for a further 15 minutes. Stir in the vinegar.

4 Increase the oven temperature to 230°C/450°F/Gas 8. Spoon the rice into the aubergine skins, top with cheese and pine nuts, return to the oven and brown for 5 minutes.

5 To make the sauce, combine the passata or tomato pulp with the curry paste, heat through and add salt to taste.

6 Spoon the sauce onto four large serving plates and position two aubergine halves on each. Garnish with basil sprigs.

Salmon Risotto with Cucumber and Tarragon

Any rice can be used for risotto, although the creamiest ones are made with short-grain arborio and carnaroli rice. Fresh tarragon and cucumber combine well to bring out the flavour of the salmon.

Serves 4

INGREDIENTS

25 g/1 oz/2 tbsp butter
1 small bunch spring onions, white
    part only, chopped
½ cucumber, peeled, deseeded
    and chopped
400 g/14 oz/2 cups short-grain
    arborio or carnaroli rice
900 ml/1½ pints/3¾ cups chicken or
    fish stock
150 ml/¼ pint/⅔ cup dry white wine
450 g/1 lb salmon fillet, skinned
    and diced
45 ml/3 tbsp chopped fresh tarragon

salmon fillet

butter

cucumber

rice

tarragon

spring onions

1 Heat the butter in a large saucepan, and add the spring onions and cucumber. Cook for 2–3 minutes without colouring.

2 Add the rice, stock and wine, return to the boil and simmer uncovered for 10 minutes, stirring occasionally.

3 Stir in the diced salmon and tarragon. Continue cooking for a further 5 minutes, then switch off the heat. Cover and leave to stand for 5 minutes before serving.

VARIATION

Long-grain rice can also be used. Choose grains that have not been pre-cooked and reduce the stock to 750 ml/1¼ pints/3⅔ cups, per 400 g/14 oz/2 cups of rice.

Green Lentil and Cabbage Salad

This warm crunchy salad makes a satisfying meal if served with crusty French bread or wholemeal rolls.

Serves 4–6

INGREDIENTS

225 g/8 oz/1 cup puy lentils
1.3 litres/2¼ pints/6 cups cold water
1 garlic clove
1 bay leaf
1 small onion, peeled and studded
    with 2 cloves
15 ml/1 tbsp olive oil
1 red onion, finely sliced
2 garlic cloves, crushed
15 ml/1 tbsp thyme leaves
350 g/12 oz cabbage, finely shredded
finely grated rind and juice of 1 lemon
15 ml/1 tbsp raspberry vinegar
salt and freshly ground black pepper

1 Rinse the lentils in cold water and place in a large pan with the water, peeled garlic clove, bay leaf and clove-studded onion. Bring to the boil and cook for 10 minutes. Reduce the heat, cover the pan and simmer gently for 15–20 minutes. Drain and remove the onion, garlic and bay leaf.

thyme

cabbage

onion

red onion

bay leaf

lemon

garlic

cloves

peppercorns

2 Heat the oil in a large pan. Add the red onion, garlic and thyme and cook for 5 minutes until softened.

3 Add the cabbage and cook for 3–5 minutes until just cooked but still crunchy.

4 Stir in the cooked lentils, lemon rind and juice and the raspberry vinegar. Season to taste and serve.

Fruit and Fibre Salad

Fresh, fast and filling, this salad makes a great starter, supper or snack.

Serves 4–6

INGREDIENTS
225 g/8 oz red or white cabbage or a
  mixture of both
3 medium carrots
1 pear
1 red-skinned eating apple
200 g/7 oz can green flageolet beans,
  drained
50 g/2 oz/¼ cup chopped dates

FOR THE DRESSING
2.5 ml/½ tsp dry English mustard
10 ml/2 tsp clear honey
30 ml/2 tbsp orange juice
5 ml/1 tsp white wine vinegar
2.5 ml/½ tsp paprika
salt and freshly ground black pepper

carrot

dates

orange

flageolet
beans

cabbage

pear

apple

1 Shred the cabbage very finely, discarding any tough stalks.

2 Cut the carrots into very thin strips, about 5 cm/2 in long.

3 Quarter, core and slice the pear and apple, leaving the skin on.

4 Put the fruit and vegetables in a bowl with the beans and dates. Mix well.

5 For the dressing, blend the mustard with the honey until smooth. Add the orange juice, vinegar, paprika and seasoning and mix well.

6 Pour the dressing over the salad and toss to coat. Chill in the refrigerator for 30 minutes before serving.

Stir-fried Chickpeas

Buy canned chickpeas and you will save all the time needed for soaking and then thoroughly cooking dried chickpeas. Served with a crisp green salad, this dish makes a filling vegetarian main course for two, or could be served in smaller quantities as a starter.

Serves 2–4 as an accompaniment

INGREDIENTS
30 ml/2 tbsp sunflower seeds
1 × 400 g/14 oz can chickpeas, drained
5 ml/1 tsp chilli powder
5 ml/1 tsp paprika
30 ml/2 tbsp vegetable oil
1 clove garlic, crushed
200 g/7 oz canned chopped tomatoes
225 g/8 oz fresh spinach, coarse stalks removed
salt and freshly ground black pepper
10 ml/2 tsp chilli oil

spinach

garlic

sunflower seeds

chickpeas

1 Heat the wok, and then add the sunflower seeds. Dry-fry until the seeds are golden and toasted.

2 Remove the sunflower seeds and set aside. Toss the chickpeas in chilli powder and paprika. Remove and reserve.

3 Heat the wok, then add the oil. When the oil is hot, stir-fry the garlic for 30 seconds, add the chickpeas and stir-fry for 1 minute.

4 Stir in the tomatoes and stir-fry for 4 minutes. Toss in the spinach, season well and stir-fry for 1 minute. Drizzle chilli oil and scatter sunflower seeds over the vegetables, then serve.

White Bean and Celery Salad

This simple bean salad is a delicious alternative to the potato salad that seems to appear on every salad menu. If you do not have time to soak and cook dried beans, use canned ones.

Serves 4

INGREDIENTS

450 g/1 lb dried white beans (haricot, canellini, navy or butter beans) or 3 × 400 g/14 oz cans white beans
1 litre/1¾ pints/4½ cups vegetable stock, made from a cube
3 stalks celery, cut into 1 cm/½ in strips
125 ml/4 fl oz French Dressing
45 ml/3 tbsp chopped fresh parsley
salt and pepper

parsley

white beans

celery

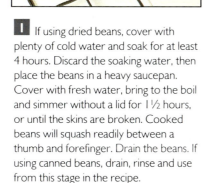

1 If using dried beans, cover with plenty of cold water and soak for at least 4 hours. Discard the soaking water, then place the beans in a heavy saucepan. Cover with fresh water, bring to the boil and simmer without a lid for 1½ hours, or until the skins are broken. Cooked beans will squash readily between a thumb and forefinger. Drain the beans. If using canned beans, drain, rinse and use from this stage in the recipe.

2 Place the cooked beans in a large saucepan. Add the vegetable stock and celery, bring to the boil, cover and simmer for 15 minutes. Drain thoroughly. Moisten the beans with the dressing and leave to cool.

3 Add the chopped parsley and season to taste with salt and pepper.

COOK'S TIP

Dried beans that have been kept for longer than 6 months will need soaking overnight to lessen their cooking time. As a rule, the less time beans have been kept in store, the shorter the soaking and cooking time they need. The times given here are suited to freshly purchased beans.

Thai Fragrant Rice

A lovely, soft, fluffy rice dish, perfumed with fresh lemon grass.

Serves 4

INGREDIENTS
1 piece of lemon grass
2 limes
225 g/8 oz/1 cup brown basmati rice
15 ml/1 tbsp olive oil
1 onion, chopped
2.5 cm/1 in piece of fresh ginger root, peeled and finely chopped
7.5 ml/1½ tsp coriander seeds
7.5 ml/1½ tsp cumin seeds
700 ml/1¼ pints/3 cups vegetable stock
60 ml/4 tbsp chopped fresh coriander
lime wedges, to serve

onion

lime

ginger

lemon grass

coriander seeds

basmati rice

cumin seeds

coriander

1 Finely chop the lemon grass.

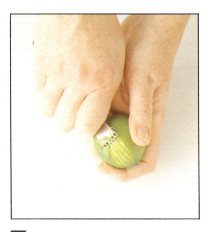

2 Remove the zest from the limes using a zester or fine grater.

3 Rinse the rice in plenty of cold water until the water runs clear. Drain through a sieve.

4 Heat the oil in a large pan and add the onion, spices, lemon grass and lime zest and cook gently for 2–3 minutes.

5 Add the rice and cook for another minute, then add the stock and bring to the boil. Reduce the heat to very low and cover the pan. Cook gently for 30 minutes then check the rice. If it is still crunchy, cover the pan again and leave for a further 3–5 minutes. Remove from the heat.

6 Stir in the fresh coriander, fluff up the grains, cover and leave for 10 minutes. Serve with lime wedges.

COOK'S TIP

Other varieties of rice, such as white basmati or long grain, can be used for this dish but you will need to adjust the cooking times accordingly.

Chinese Jewelled Rice

This rice dish, with its many different, interesting ingredients, can make a meal in itself.

Serves 4

INGREDIENTS

350 g/12 oz long grain rice
45 ml/3 tbsp vegetable oil
1 onion, roughly chopped
115 g/4 oz cooked ham, diced
175 g/6 oz canned white crabmeat
75 g/3 oz canned water chestnuts,
    drained and cut into cubes
4 dried black Chinese mushrooms,
    soaked, drained and cut into dice
115 g/4 oz peas, thawed if frozen
30 ml/2 tbsp oyster sauce
5 ml/1 tsp sugar

rice

Chinese mushrooms

diced ham

water chestnuts

peas

crabmeat

1 Rinse the rice, then cook for 10–12 minutes in 700–850 ml/1¼–1½ pints water in a saucepan with a tight-fitting lid. When cooked, refresh under cold water. Heat the wok, then add half the oil. When the oil is hot, stir-fry the rice for 3 minutes, then remove and set aside.

2 Add the remaining oil to the wok. When the oil is hot, cook the onion until softened but not coloured.

3 Add all the remaining ingredients and stir-fry for 2 minutes.

4 Return the rice to the wok and stir-fry for 3 minutes, then serve.

Took a lot of preparation. Was very boring to eat

Nutty Rice and Mushroom Stir-fry

This delicious and substantial supper dish can be eaten hot or cold with salads.

Serves 4–6

INGREDIENTS
350 g/12 oz long grain rice
45 ml/3 tbsp sunflower oil
1 small onion, roughly chopped
225 g/8 oz field mushrooms, sliced
50 g/2 oz/½ cup hazelnuts, roughly chopped
50 g/2 oz/½ cup pecan nuts, roughly chopped
50 g/2 oz/½ cup almonds, roughly chopped
60 ml/4 tbsp fresh parsley, chopped
salt and freshly ground black pepper

rice

almonds

field mushroom

hazelnuts

pecan nuts

1 Rinse the rice, then cook for 10–12 minutes in 700–850 ml/1¼–1½ pints water in a saucepan with a tight-fitting lid. When cooked, refresh under cold water. Heat the wok, then add half the oil. When the oil is hot, stir-fry the rice for 2–3 minutes. Remove and set aside.

2 Add the remaining oil and stir-fry the onion for 2 minutes until softened.

3 Mix in the field mushrooms and stir-fry for 2 minutes.

4 Add all the nuts and stir-fry for 1 minute. Return the rice to the wok and stir-fry for 3 minutes. Season with salt and pepper. Stir in the parsley and serve.

Jamaican Spiced Cod Steaks with Pumpkin Ragout

Spicy hot from Kingston town, this fast fish dish is guaranteed to appeal. The term 'ragout' is taken from the old French verb ragoûter, which means to stimulate the appetite.

Serves 4

INGREDIENTS
finely grated zest of ½ orange
30 ml/2 tbsp black peppercorns
15 ml/1 tbsp allspice berries or
  Jamaican pepper
2.5 ml/½ tsp salt
4 × 175 g/6 oz cod steaks
groundnut oil, for frying
new potatoes, to serve (optional)
45 ml/3 tbsp chopped fresh parsley,
  to garnish

FOR THE RAGOUT
30 ml/2 tbsp groundnut oil
1 medium onion, chopped
2.5 cm/1 in fresh root ginger, peeled
  and grated
450 g/1 lb fresh pumpkin, peeled,
  deseeded and chopped
3–4 shakes of Tabasco sauce
30 ml/2 tbsp soft brown sugar
15 ml/1 tbsp vinegar

pumpkin

cod steaks

ginger

COOK'S TIP

This recipe can be adapted using any type of firm pink or white fish that is available, such as haddock, whiting, monkfish, halibut or tuna.

1 To make the ragout, heat the oil in a heavy saucepan and add the onion and ginger. Cover and cook, stirring, for 3–4 minutes until soft.

2 Add the chopped pumpkin, Tabasco sauce, brown sugar and vinegar, cover and cook over a low heat for 10–12 minutes until softened.

3 Combine the orange zest, peppercorns, allspice or Jamaican pepper and salt, then crush coarsely using a pestle and mortar. (Alternatively, coarsely grind the peppercorns in a pepper mill and combine with the zest and seasoning.)

4 Scatter the spice mixture over both sides of the fish and moisten with a sprinkling of oil.

5 Heat a large frying pan and fry the cod steaks for 12 minutes, turning once.

6 Serve the cod steaks with a spoonful of pumpkin ragout and new potatoes, if desired, and garnish the ragout with chopped fresh parsley.

Pickled Herrings with Beetroot and Apple Relish

Soused or pickled herrings are delicious with cooked beetroot. Serve with buttered rye bread and a sweet and sour apple relish.

Serves 4

INGREDIENTS
2 eggs
8 pickled herrings
250 g/9 oz cooked baby beetroot
fresh flat-leaf parsley, to garnish
4 slices buttered rye bread, to serve

FOR THE RELISH
30 ml/2 tbsp vegetable oil
2 large eating apples, peeled, cored
   and finely chopped
1 medium onion, chopped
15 ml/1 tbsp sugar
15 ml/1 tbsp cider vinegar
5 ml/1 tsp hot mustard
pinch of salt

pickled herrings   *eggs*

baby beetroot

onion   *apples*

1 Bring a saucepan of water to the boil, gently lower in the eggs and cook for 10 minutes. Cool under running water and peel. Cut into quarters.

2 To make the relish, heat the oil in a saucepan and add the apple and onion. Cook over a gentle heat for 3–4 minutes without colouring. Add the sugar, vinegar and mustard, then season with salt.

3 Divide the herrings between four plates. Slice the beetroot and arrange to one side with the relish. Decorate with egg quarters and garnish with parsley. Serve with buttered rye bread.

COOK'S TIP
Choose full-flavoured green or red apples for the best results.

Dover Sole in a Green Parsley Jacket

Quick to prepare and absolutely delicious, nothing compares with the rich sweetness of a Dover sole. Here, this fine fish sports a green parsley jacket trimmed with lemon and a hint of garlic.

Serves 2

INGREDIENTS
350 g/12 oz floury potatoes, peeled and finely chopped
300 ml/½ pint/1¼ cups skimmed milk, or as required
pinch of grated nutmeg
2 × Dover sole, skinned
25 g/1 oz/2 tbsp butter
salt and freshly ground black pepper
lemon wedges, to serve

FOR THE PARSLEY JACKET
25 g/1 oz/½ cup fresh parsley
25 g/1 oz crustless white bread, cubed
45 ml/3 tbsp milk
30 ml/2 tbsp olive oil
finely grated zest of ½ small lemon
1 small garlic clove, crushed

1 In a non-stick saucepan, cover the potatoes with the milk, add salt to taste, and the nutmeg, and bring to the boil. Simmer, uncovered, for 15 minutes until the potatoes have absorbed the milk. Mash, cover and keep warm.

Dover sole

lemon

parsley

2 To make the parsley jacket, chop the parsley in a food processor. Add the bread, milk, olive oil, lemon zest and garlic, then reduce to a fine paste.

3 Preheat a moderate grill. Season the sole, dot with butter and grill for 5 minutes. Turn and allow 2 minutes on the other side. Spread with the parsley mixture, return to the grill and continue to cook for a further 5 minutes. Serve with the mashed potatoes and wedges of lemon.

VARIATION
The same parsley mixture can be used to cover fillets of cod, haddock, whiting or silver hake.

Herby Fishcakes with Lemon and Chive Sauce

The wonderful flavour of fresh herbs makes these fishcakes the catch of the day.

Serves 4

INGREDIENTS
350 g/12 oz potatoes, peeled
75 ml/5 tbsp skimmed milk
350 g/12 oz haddock or hoki fillets, skinned
15 ml/1 tbsp lemon juice
15 ml/1 tbsp creamed horseradish sauce
30 ml/2 tbsp chopped fresh parsley
flour, for dusting
115 g/4 oz/2 cups fresh wholemeal breadcrumbs
salt and freshly ground black pepper
sprig of flat-leaf parsley, to garnish
mange tout and a sliced tomato and onion salad, to serve

FOR THE LEMON AND CHIVE SAUCE
thinly pared rind and juice of ½ small lemon
120 ml/4 fl oz/½ cup dry white wine
2 thin slices fresh root ginger
10 ml/2 tsp cornflour
30 ml/2 tbsp snipped fresh chives

chives

potatoes

haddock

lemon

ginger

breadcrumbs

parsley

1 Cook the potatoes in a large saucepan of boiling water for 15-20 minutes. Drain and mash with the milk and season to taste.

2 Purée the fish together with the lemon juice and horseradish sauce in a blender or food processor. Mix together with the potatoes and parsley.

3 With floured hands, shape the mixture into eight fishcakes and coat with the breadcrumbs. Chill in the refrigerator for 30 minutes.

4 Cook the fishcakes under a pre-heated moderate grill for 5 minutes on each side, until browned.

5 To make the sauce, cut the lemon rind into julienne strips and put into a large saucepan together with the lemon juice, wine and ginger and season to taste.

6 Simmer uncovered for 6 minutes. Blend the cornflour with 15 ml/1 tbsp of cold water. Add to the saucepan and simmer until clear. Stir in the chives immediately before serving. Serve the sauce hot with the fishcakes, garnished with sprigs of flat-leaf parsley and accompanied with mange tout and a sliced tomato and onion salad.

Butterfly Prawns

Use raw prawns if you can because the flavour will be better, but if you substitute cooked prawns, cut down the stir-fry cooking time by one third.

Serves 4

INGREDIENTS
2.5 cm/1 in piece root ginger
350 g/12 oz raw prawns, thawed if
    frozen
50 g/2 oz/½ cup raw peanuts, roughly
    chopped
45 ml/3 tbsp vegetable oil
1 clove garlic, crushed
1 red chilli, finely chopped
45 ml/3 tbsp smooth peanut butter
15 ml/1 tbsp fresh coriander, chopped
fresh coriander sprigs, to garnish

FOR THE DRESSING
150 ml/¼ pint/⅔ cup natural
    low fat yogurt
5 cm/2 in piece cucumber, diced
salt and freshly ground black pepper

diced cucumber

peanuts

prawn

coriander

chilli

1 To make the dressing, mix together the yogurt, cucumber and seasoning in a bowl, then leave to chill while preparing and cooking the prawns.

2 Peel the ginger, and chop it finely.

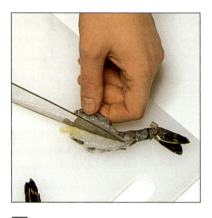

3 Prepare the prawns by peeling off the shells, leaving the tails intact. Make a slit down the back of each prawn and remove the black vein, then slit the prawn completely down the back and open it out to make a 'butterfly'.

4 Heat the wok and dry-fry the peanuts, stirring constantly until golden brown. Leave to cool. Wipe out the wok with kitchen towels.

5 Heat the wok, add the oil and when hot add the ginger, garlic and chilli. Stir-fry for 2–3 minutes until the garlic is softened but not brown.

6 Add the prawns, then increase the heat and stir-fry for 1–2 minutes until the prawns turn pink. Stir in the peanut butter and stir-fry for 2 minutes. Add the chopped coriander, then scatter in the peanuts. Garnish with coriander sprigs and serve with the cucumber dressing.

Cajun-style Cod

This recipe works equally well with any firm-fleshed fish such as swordfish, shark, tuna or halibut.

Serves 4

INGREDIENTS
4 cod steaks, each weighing about
    175 g/6 oz
30 ml/2 tbsp natural low fat yogurt
15 ml/1 tbsp lime or lemon juice
1 garlic clove, crushed
5 ml/1 tsp ground cumin
5 ml/1 tsp paprika
5 ml/1 tsp mustard powder
2.5 ml/½ tsp cayenne pepper
2.5 ml/½ tsp dried thyme
2.5 ml/½ tsp dried oregano
new potatoes and a mixed salad,
    to serve

cod

lime

mustard powder

thyme

paprika

1 Pat the fish dry on absorbent kitchen paper. Mix together the yogurt and lime or lemon juice and brush lightly over both sides of the fish.

2 Mix together the garlic clove, spices and herbs. Coat both sides of the fish with the seasoning mix, rubbing in well.

COOK'S TIP

If you don't have a ridged grill pan, heat several metal skewers under a grill until red hot. Holding the ends with a cloth, press onto the seasoned fish before cooking to give a ridged appearance.

3 Spray a ridged grill pan or heavy-based frying pan with non-stick cooking spray. Heat until very hot. Add the fish and cook over a high heat for 4 minutes, or until the underside is well browned.

4 Turn over and cook for a further 4 minutes, or until the steaks have cooked through. Serve immediately accompanied with new potatoes and a mixed salad.

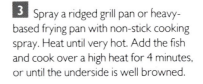

Plaice Provençal

Re-create the taste of the Mediterranean with this easy-to-make fish casserole.

Serves 4

INGREDIENTS
4 large plaice fillets
2 small red onions
120 ml/4 fl oz/½ cup vegetable stock
60 ml/4 tbsp dry red wine
1 garlic clove, crushed
2 courgettes, sliced
1 yellow pepper, seeded and sliced
400 g/14 oz can chopped tomatoes
15 ml/1 tbsp chopped fresh thyme
salt and freshly ground black pepper

chopped tomatoes

plaice

thyme

courgettes

red onion

pepper

1 Pre-heat the oven to 180°C/350°F/Gas 4. Skin the plaice with a sharp knife by laying it skin-side down. Holding the tail end, push the knife between the skin and flesh in a sawing movement. Hold the knife at a slight angle with the blade towards the skin.

2 Cut each onion into eight wedges. Put into a heavy-based saucepan with the stock. Cover and simmer for 5 minutes. Uncover and continue to cook, stirring occasionally, until the stock has reduced entirely. Add the wine and garlic clove to the pan and continue to cook until the onions are soft.

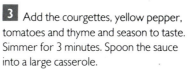

3 Add the courgettes, yellow pepper, tomatoes and thyme and season to taste. Simmer for 3 minutes. Spoon the sauce into a large casserole.

4 Fold each fillet in half and place on top of the sauce. Cover and cook in the pre-heated oven for 15-20 minutes until the fish is opaque and cooked.

Grilled Snapper with Hot Mango Salsa

A ripe mango provides the basis for a deliciously rich fruity salsa. The dressing needs no oil and features the tropical flavours of coriander, ginger and chilli.

Serves 4

INGREDIENTS

350 g/12 oz new potatoes
3 eggs
115 g/4 oz French beans, topped, tailed and halved
4 × 350 g/12 oz red snapper, scaled and gutted
30 ml/2 tbsp olive oil
175 g/6 oz mixed lettuce leaves, such as frisée or Webb's
2 cherry tomatoes
salt and freshly ground black pepper

FOR THE SALSA

45 ml/3 tbsp chopped fresh coriander
1 medium sized ripe mango, peeled, stoned and diced
½ red chilli, deseeded and chopped
2.5 cm/1 in fresh root ginger, grated
juice of 2 limes
generous pinch of celery salt

French beans

red snapper

mango *ginger*

chilli

1 Bring the potatoes to the boil in a large saucepan of salted water and simmer for 15–20 minutes. Drain.

2 Bring a second large saucepan of salted water to the boil. Put in the eggs and boil for 4 minutes, then add the beans and cook for a further 6 minutes, so that the eggs have had a total of 10 minutes. Remove the eggs from the pan, cool, peel and cut into quarters.

4 To make the dressing, place the coriander in a food processor. Add the mango, chilli, ginger, lime juice and celery salt and process smoothly.

5 Moisten the lettuce leaves with olive oil, and distribute them between four large plates.

VARIATION

If fresh mangoes are unavailable, use the canned variety and drain well. Sea bream are also good served with the hot mango salsa.

3 Preheat a moderate grill. Slash each snapper three times on either side moisten with oil and cook for 12 minutes, turning once.

6 Arrange the snapper over the lettuce and season to taste. Halve the new potatoes and tomatoes, and distribute them with the beans and quartered hard-boiled eggs over the salad. Serve with the salsa dressing.

Marinated Monkfish and Mussel Skewers

You can cook these fish kebabs on the barbecue – when the weather allows!

Serves 4

INGREDIENTS
450 g/1 lb monkfish, skinned and
  boned
5 ml/1 tsp olive oil
30 ml/2 tbsp lemon juice
5 ml/1 tsp paprika
1 garlic clove, crushed
4 turkey rashers
8 cooked mussels
8 raw prawns
15 ml/1 tbsp chopped fresh dill
salt and freshly ground black pepper
lemon wedges, to garnish
salad leaves and long-grain and wild
  rice, to serve

mussels

turkey rashers

dill

lemon

monkfish

1 Cut the monkfish into 2.5 cm/1 in cubes and place in a shallow glass dish. Mix together the oil, lemon juice, paprika, and garlic clove and season with pepper.

2 Pour the marinade over the fish and toss to coat evenly. Cover and leave in a cool place for 30 minutes.

COOK'S TIP

Monkfish is ideal for kebabs, but can be expensive. Cod or hake are good alternatives.

3 Cut the turkey rashers in half and wrap each strip around a mussel. Thread onto skewers alternating with the fish cubes and raw prawns.

4 Cook the kebabs under a hot grill for 7-8 minutes, turning once and basting with the marinade. Sprinkle with chopped dill and salt. Garnish with lemon wedges and serve with salad and rice.

Pasta with Spinach and Anchovy Sauce

Deliciously earthy, this would make a good starter or light supper dish. Add some sultanas (golden raisins) to ring the changes!

Serves 4

INGREDIENTS

900 g/2 lb fresh spinach or 550 g/
  1¼ lb frozen leaf spinach, thawed
450 g/1 lb/4 cups angel hair pasta
salt
60 ml/4 tbsp olive oil
45 ml/3 tbsp pine nuts
2 garlic cloves, crushed
6 canned anchovy fillets or whole
  salted anchovies, drained and
  chopped
butter, for tossing the pasta

olive oil

pine nuts

spinach

anchovy fillets

garlic   *angel hair pasta*

1 Wash the spinach well and remove the tough stalks. Drain thoroughly. Place in a large saucepan with only the water that still clings to the leaves. Cover with a lid and cook over a high heat, shaking the pan occasionally, until the spinach is just wilted and still bright green. Drain.

2 Cook the pasta in plenty of boiling salted water according to the manufacturer's instructions.

3 Heat the oil in a saucepan and fry the pine nuts until golden. Remove with a perforated spoon. Add the garlic to the oil in the pan and fry until golden. Add the anchovies.

4 Stir in the spinach and cook for 2–3 minutes or until heated through. Stir in the pine nuts. Drain the pasta, toss in a little butter and turn into a warmed serving bowl. Top with the sauce and fork through roughly.

Smoked Trout Cannelloni

Smoked trout can be bought already filleted or whole. If you buy fillets, you'll need 225 g/8 oz of fish.

Serves 4–6

INGREDIENTS
1 large onion, finely chopped
1 garlic clove, crushed
60 ml/4 tbsp vegetable stock
2 × 400 g/14 oz cans chopped
    tomatoes
2.5 ml/½ tsp dried mixed herbs
1 smoked trout, weighing about
    400 g/14 oz
75 g/3 oz/¾ cup frozen peas, thawed
75 g/3 oz/1½ cups fresh breadcrumbs
16 cannelloni tubes
salt and freshly ground black pepper
mixed salad, to serve

FOR THE CHEESE SAUCE
25 g/1 oz/2 tbsp low fat spread
25 g/1 oz/¼ cup plain flour
350 ml/12 fl oz/1½ cups
    skimmed milk
freshly grated nutmeg
15 g/½ oz/1½ tbsp freshly grated
    Parmesan cheese

mixed herbs

trout

onion

tomato

chopped tomatoes   *cannelloni*

1 Simmer the onion, garlic clove and stock in a large covered saucepan for 3 minutes. Uncover and continue to cook, stirring occasionally, until the stock has reduced entirely.

2 Stir in the tomatoes and dried herbs. Simmer uncovered for a further 10 minutes, or until very thick.

3 Meanwhile, skin the smoked trout with a sharp knife. Carefully flake the flesh and discard all the bones. Mix the fish together with the tomato mixture, peas, breadcrumbs, salt and freshly ground black pepper.

4 Pre-heat the oven to 190°C/375°F/Gas 5. Spoon the filling into the cannelloni tubes and arrange in an ovenproof dish.

5 For the sauce, put the low fat spread, flour and milk into a saucepan and cook over a medium heat, whisking constantly until the sauce thickens. Simmer for 2-3 minutes, stirring all the time. Season to taste with salt, freshly ground black pepper and nutmeg.

COOK'S TIP

You can use a 220 g/7 oz can of tuna in brine in place of the trout, if preferred.

6 Pour the sauce over the cannelloni and sprinkle with the grated Parmesan cheese. Bake in the pre-heated oven for 35-40 minutes, or until the top is golden and bubbling. Serve with a mixed salad.

79

Spaghetti with Tomato and Clam Sauce

Small sweet clams make this a delicately succulent sauce. Cockles would make a good substitute, or even mussels. Don't be tempted to use seafood pickled in vinegar – the result will be inedible!

Serves 4

INGREDIENTS
900 g/2 lb live small clams, or 2 × 400 g/14 oz cans clams in brine, drained
90 ml/6 tbsp olive oil
2 garlic cloves, crushed
600 g/1 lb 5 oz canned chopped tomatoes
45 ml/3 tbsp chopped fresh parsley
salt and pepper
450 g/1 lb spaghetti

olive oil *spaghetti*

parsley

garlic

clams

1 If using live clams, place them in a bowl of cold water and rinse several times to remove any grit or sand. Drain.

2 Heat the oil in a saucepan and add the clams. Stir over a high heat until the clams open. Throw away any that do not open. Transfer the clams to a bowl with a perforated spoon.

3 Reduce the clam juice left in the pan to almost nothing by boiling fast; this will also concentrate the flavour. Add the garlic and fry until golden. Pour in the tomatoes, bring to the boil and cook for 3–4 minutes until reduced. Stir in the clam mixture or canned clams and half the parsley and heat through. Season.

4 Cook the pasta in plenty of boiling salted water according to the manufacturer's instructions. Drain well and turn into a warm serving dish. Pour over the sauce and sprinkle with the remaining parsley.

Pasta with Tuna, Capers and Anchovies

This piquant sauce could be made without the addition of tomatoes – just heat the oil, add the other ingredients and heat through gently before tossing with the pasta.

Serves 4

INGREDIENTS
400 g/14 oz canned tuna fish in oil
30 ml/2 tbsp olive oil
2 garlic cloves, crushed
800 g/1¾ lb canned chopped
    tomatoes
6 canned anchovy fillets, drained
30 ml/2 tbsp capers in vinegar,
    drained
30 ml/2 tbsp chopped fresh basil
salt and pepper
450 g/1 lb/4 cups rigatoni, penne or
    garganelle
sprigs fresh basil, to garnish

olive oil

rigatoni

tuna fish

basil

anchovy fillets

capers

garlic

1 Drain the oil from the tuna into a saucepan, add the olive oil and heat gently until it stops 'spitting'.

2 Add the garlic and fry until golden. Stir in the tomatoes and simmer for 25 minutes until thickened.

3 Flake the tuna and cut the anchovies in half. Stir into the sauce with the capers and chopped basil. Season well.

4 Cook the pasta in plenty of boiling salted water according to the manufacturer's instructions. Drain well and toss with the sauce. Garnish with fresh basil sprigs.

Seafood Pasta Shells with Spinach Sauce

You'll need very large pasta shells, measuring about 4 cm/1½ in long for this dish; don't try stuffing smaller shells – they're much too fiddly!

Serves 4

INGREDIENTS

15 g/½ oz/1 tbsp low fat spread
8 spring onions, finely sliced
6 tomatoes
32 large dried pasta shells
225 g/8 oz/1 cup low fat soft cheese
90 ml/6 tbsp skimmed milk
pinch of freshly grated nutmeg
225 g/8 oz prawns
175 g/6 oz can white crabmeat, drained and flaked
115 g/4 oz frozen chopped spinach, thawed and drained
salt and freshly ground black pepper

spring onions

prawns

pasta shells

crabmeat

spinach

tomatoes

1 Pre-heat the oven to 150°C/300°F/ Gas 2. Melt the low fat spread in a small saucepan and gently cook the spring onions for 3-4 minutes, or until softened.

2 Plunge the tomatoes into a saucepan of boiling water for 1 minute, then into a saucepan of cold water. Slip off the skins. Halve the tomatoes, remove the seeds and cores and roughly chop the flesh.

3 Cook the pasta shells in lightly salted boiling water for about 10 minutes, or until *al dente*. Drain well.

4 Put the low fat soft cheese and skimmed milk into a saucepan and heat gently, stirring until blended. Season with salt, freshly ground black pepper and a pinch of nutmeg. Measure 30 ml/2 tbsp of the sauce into a bowl.

5 Add the spring onions, tomatoes, prawns, and crabmeat to the bowl. Mix well. Spoon the filling into the shells and place in a single layer in a shallow ovenproof dish. Cover with foil and cook in the pre-heated oven for 10 minutes.

6 Stir the spinach into the remaining sauce. Bring to the boil and simmer gently for 1 minute, stirring all the time. Drizzle over the pasta shells and serve hot.

Grilled Salmon and Spring Vegetable Salad

Spring is the time to enjoy sweet young vegetables. Cook them briefly, cool to room temperature, dress and serve with a piece of lightly grilled salmon topped with sorrel and quails' eggs.

quails' eggs

new potatoes

patty pan squash

sorrel

sugar-snap peas

salmon

green beans

baby sweetcorn

carrots

Serves 4

INGREDIENTS
350 g/12 oz small new potatoes, scrubbed or scraped
4 quails' eggs
115 g/4 oz young carrots, peeled
115 g/4 oz baby sweetcorn
115 g/4 oz sugar-snap peas, topped and tailed
115 g/4 oz fine green beans, topped and tailed
115 g/4 oz young courgettes
115 g/4 oz patty pan squash (optional)

100 ml/4 fl oz French dressing
4 salmon fillets, each weighing 150 g/5 oz, skinned
115 g/4 oz sorrel or young spinach, stems removed
salt and freshly ground black pepper

1 Bring the potatoes to the boil in salted water and cook for 15–20 minutes. Drain, cover and keep warm.

2 Cover the quails' eggs with boiling water and cook for 8 minutes. Refresh under cold water, shell and cut in half.

3 Bring a saucepan of salted water to the boil, add all the vegetables and cook for 2–3 minutes. Drain well. Place the hot vegetables and potatoes in a salad bowl, moisten with French dressing and allow to cool.

4 Brush the salmon fillets with French dressing and grill for 6 minutes, turning once.

5 Place the sorrel in a stainless-steel or enamel saucepan with 60 ml/2 tbsp French dressing, cover and soften over a gentle heat for 2 minutes. Strain in a small sieve and cool to room temperature.

6 Divide the potatoes and vegetables between 4 large plates, then position a piece of salmon in the centre of each. Finally place a spoonful of sorrel on each piece of salmon and top with a halved quails' egg. Season and serve at room temperature.

Avocado, Crab and Coriander Salad

The sweet richness of crab combines especially well with ripe avocado, fresh coriander and tomato.

Serves 4

INGREDIENTS
700 g/1½ lb small new potatoes
1 sprig fresh mint
900 g/2 lb boiled crabs, or 275 g/10 oz frozen crab meat
1 Batavian endive or butterhead lettuce
175 g/6 oz lamb's lettuce or young spinach
1 large ripe avocado, peeled and sliced
175 g/6 oz cherry tomatoes
salt, pepper and nutmeg

DRESSING
75 ml/5 tbsp olive oil, preferably Tuscan
15 ml/1 tbsp lime juice
45 ml/3 tbsp chopped fresh coriander
½ tsp caster sugar

crab

avocado

mint

cherry tomatoes

lamb's lettuce

coriander

new potatoes

1 Scrape or peel the potatoes. Cover with water, add a good pinch of salt and a sprig of mint. Bring to the boil and simmer for 20 minutes. Drain, cover and keep warm until needed.

2 Remove the legs and claws from each crab. Crack these open with the back of a chopping knife and then remove the white meat.

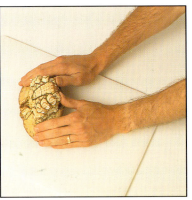

3 Turn the crab on its back and push the rear leg section away with the thumb and forefinger of each hand. Remove the flesh from inside the shell.

4 Discard the soft gills ('dead men's fingers'): the crab uses these gills to filter impurities in its diet. Apart from these and the shell, everything else is edible – white and dark meat.

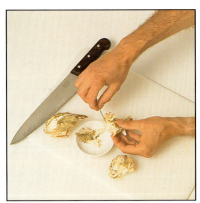

5 Split the central body section open with a knife and remove the white and dark flesh with a pick or skewer.

COOK'S TIP

Young crabs offer the sweetest meat, but are more fiddly to prepare than older, larger ones. The hen crab carries more flesh than the cock which is considered to have a better overall flavour. The cock crab, shown here, is identified by his narrow apron flap at the rear. The hen has a broad flap under which she carries her eggs. Frozen crab meat is a good alternative to fresh and retains much of its original sweetness.

6 Combine the dressing ingredients in a screw-top jar and shake. Wash and spin the lettuces, then dress them. Distribute between 4 plates. Top with avocado, crab, tomatoes and warm new potatoes. Season with salt, pepper and freshly grated nutmeg and serve.

Pasta, Melon and Prawn Salad

Orange-fleshed cantaloupe or Charentais melon looks spectacular in this salad. You could also use a mixture of ogen, cantaloupe and water melon.

Serves 4–6

INGREDIENTS
175 g/6 oz/1½ cups pasta shapes
225 g/8 oz frozen prawns
   thawed and drained
1 large or 2 small melons
60 ml/4 tbsp olive oil
15 ml/1 tbsp tarragon vinegar
30 ml/2 tbsp chopped fresh chives or
   parsley
sprigs of herbs, to garnish
shredded Chinese leaves, to serve

melons

pasta shapes

prawns

Chinese leaves

1 Cook the pasta in boiling salted water according to the manufacturer's instructions. Drain well and allow to cool.

2 Peel the prawns and discard the shells.

3 Halve the melon and remove the seeds with a teaspoon. Carefully scoop the flesh into balls with a melon baller and mix with the prawns and pasta.

4 Whisk the oil, vinegar and chopped herbs together. Pour on to the prawn mixture and turn to coat. Cover and chill for at least 30 minutes.

5 Meanwhile shred the Chinese leaves and use to line a shallow bowl or the empty melon halves.

6 Pile the prawn mixture on to the Chinese leaves and garnish with herbs.

Tuna Fish and Flageolet Bean Salad

Two cans of tuna fish form the basis of this delicious store cupboard salad.

Serves 4

INGREDIENTS
90 ml/6 tbsp low fat mayonnaise
5 ml/1 tsp mustard
30 ml/2 tbsp capers
45 ml/3 tbsp chopped fresh parsley
pinch of celery salt
2 × 200 g/7 oz cans tuna fish in oil, drained
3 little gem lettuces
1 × 400 g/14 oz can flageolet beans, drained
1 × 400 g/14 oz can baby artichoke hearts, halved
12 cherry tomatoes, halved
toasted sesame bread, to serve

tomatoes

parsley

little gem lettuce

artichoke hearts

mustard

capers

tuna fish

flageolet beans

1 Combine the mayonnaise, mustard, capers and parsley in a mixing bowl. Season to taste with celery salt. Flake the tuna into the dressing and toss gently.

2 Arrange the lettuce leaves on four plates, then spoon the tuna mixture onto the leaves.

3 Spoon the flageolet beans to one side, followed by the tomatoes and artichoke hearts. Serve with slices of toasted sesame bread.

VARIATION
Flageolet beans are taken from the under-developed pods of haricot beans. They have a sweet creamy flavour and an attractive green colour. If not available, use white haricot or cannellini beans.

Smoked Trout and Horseradish Salad

Salads are the easy answer to fast, healthy eating. When lettuce is sweet and crisp, partner it with fillets of smoked trout, warm new potatoes and a creamy horseradish dressing.

Serves 4

INGREDIENTS

675 g/1½ lb new potatoes
4 smoked trout fillets
115 g/4 oz mixed lettuce leaves
4 slices dark rye bread, cut into
   fingers
salt and freshly ground black pepper

FOR THE DRESSING

60 ml/4 tbsp creamed horseradish
60 ml/4 tbsp groundnut oil
15 ml/1 tbsp white wine vinegar
10 ml/2 tsp caraway seeds

rye bread

new potatoes

caraway seeds

horseradish

smoked trout fillets

lettuce leaves

1 Bring the potatoes to the boil in a saucepan of salted water and simmer for 20 minutes. Remove the skin from the trout, and lift the flesh from the bone.

2 To make the dressing, place all the ingredients in a screw-topped jar and shake vigorously. Season the lettuce leaves and moisten them with the prepared dressing. Distribute between four plates.

3 Flake the trout fillets and halve the potatoes. Scatter them together with the rye fingers over the salad leaves and toss to mix. Season to taste and serve.

COOK'S TIP

To save time washing lettuce leaves, buy them ready-prepared from your supermarket. It is better to season the leaves rather than the dressing when making a salad.

Indonesian-style Satay Chicken

Use boneless chicken thighs to give a good flavour to these satays.

Serves 4

INGREDIENTS
50 g/2 oz/½ cup raw peanuts
45 ml/3 tbsp vegetable oil
1 small onion, finely chopped
2.5 cm/1 in piece root ginger, peeled
 and finely chopped
1 clove garlic, crushed
675 g/1½ lb chicken thighs, skinned
 and cut into cubes
90 g/3½ oz creamed coconut,
 roughly chopped
15 ml/1 tbsp chilli sauce
60 ml/4 tbsp crunchy peanut butter
5 ml/1 tsp soft dark brown sugar
150 ml/¼ pint/⅔ cup skimmed milk
¼ tsp salt

creamed coconut

peanuts

chilli sauce

peanut butter

COOK'S TIP
Soak bamboo skewers in cold water for at least 2 hours, or preferably overnight, so they do not char when keeping the threaded chicken warm in the oven.

1 Shell and rub the skins from the peanuts, then soak them in enough water to cover, for 1 minute. Drain the nuts and cut them into slivers.

2 Heat the wok and add 5 ml/1 tsp oil. When the oil is hot, stir-fry the peanuts for 1 minute until crisp and golden. Remove with a slotted spoon and drain on kitchen towels.

3 Add the remaining oil to the hot wok. When the oil is hot, add the onion, ginger and garlic and stir-fry for 2–3 minutes until softened but not browned. Remove with a slotted spoon and drain on kitchen towels.

4 Add the chicken pieces and stir-fry for 3–4 minutes until crisp and golden on all sides. Thread on to pre-soaked bamboo skewers and keep warm.

5 Add the creamed coconut to the hot wok in small pieces and stir-fry until melted. Add the chilli sauce, peanut butter and cooked ginger and garlic, and simmer for 2 minutes. Stir in the sugar, milk and salt, and simmer for a further 3 minutes. Serve the skewered chicken hot, with a dish of the hot dipping sauce sprinkled with the roasted peanuts.

Chicken Teriyaki

A bowl of boiled rice is the ideal accompaniment to this Japanese-style chicken dish.

Serves 4

INGREDIENTS
450 g/1 lb boneless, skinless
  chicken breasts
orange segments and mustard and
  cress, to garnish

FOR THE MARINADE
5 ml/1 tsp sugar
15 ml/1 tbsp rice wine
15 ml/1 tbsp dry sherry
30 ml/2 tbsp dark soy sauce
rind of 1 orange, grated

orange

rice wine

soy sauce

chicken breast

1 Finely slice the chicken.

2 Mix all the marinade ingredients together in a bowl.

COOK'S TIP

Make sure the marinade is brought to the boil and cooked for 4–5 minutes, because it has been in contact with raw chicken.

3 Place the chicken in a bowl, pour over the marinade and leave to marinate for 15 minutes.

4 Heat the wok, add the chicken and marinade and stir-fry for 4–5 minutes. Serve garnished with orange segments and mustard and cress.

Stir-fried Sweet and Sour Chicken

There are few cookery concepts that are better suited to today's busy lifestyle than the all-in-one stir-fry. This one has a South-east Asian influence.

Serves 4

INGREDIENTS
275 g/10 oz Chinese egg noodles
30 ml/2 tbsp vegetable oil
3 spring onions, chopped
1 garlic clove, crushed
2.5 cm/1 in fresh root ginger, peeled
   and grated
5 ml/1 tsp hot paprika
5 ml/1 tsp ground coriander
3 boneless chicken breasts, sliced
115 g/4 oz/1 cup sugar-snap peas,
   topped and tailed
115 g/4 oz baby sweetcorn, halved
225 g/8 oz fresh beansprouts
15 ml/1 tbsp cornflour
45 ml/3 tbsp soy sauce
45 ml/3 tbsp lemon juice
15 ml/1 tbsp sugar
45 ml/3 tbsp chopped fresh coriander
   or spring onion tops, to garnish

COOK'S TIP
Large wok lids are cumbersome and can be difficult to store in a small kitchen. Consider placing a circle of greaseproof paper against the food surface to keep cooking juices in.

1 Bring a large saucepan of salted water to the boil. Add the noodles and cook according to the packet instructions. Drain, cover and keep warm.

chicken breasts

garlic

spring onions

paprika

egg noodles

soy sauce

sugar-snap peas

ginger

2 Heat the oil. Add the spring onions and cook over a gentle heat. Mix in the next five ingredients, then stir-fry for 3–4 minutes. Add the next three ingredients and steam briefly. Add the noodles.

3 Combine the cornflour, soy sauce, lemon juice and sugar in a small bowl. Add to the wok and simmer briefly to thicken. Serve garnished with chopped coriander or spring onion tops.

Lemon Chicken Stir-fry

It is essential to prepare all the ingredients before you begin so they are ready to cook. This dish is cooked in minutes.

Serves 4

INGREDIENTS
4 boned and skinned chicken breasts
15 ml/1 tbsp light soy sauce
75 ml/5 tbsp cornflour
1 bunch spring onions
1 lemon
1 garlic clove, crushed
15 ml/1 tbsp caster sugar
30 ml/2 tbsp sherry
150 ml/¼ pint/⅔ cup chicken stock
60 ml/4 tbsp olive oil
salt and freshly ground black pepper

caster sugar

garlic

olive oil   spring onions

lemon

soy sauce

cornflour

chicken breasts

1 Divide the chicken breasts into two natural fillets. Place each between two sheets of clear film and flatten to a thickness of 5 mm/¼ in with a rolling pin.

2 Cut into 2.5 cm/1 in strips across the grain of the fillets. Put the chicken into a bowl with the soy sauce and toss to coat. Sprinkle over 60 ml/4 tbsp cornflour to coat each piece.

3 Trim the roots off the spring onions and cut diagonally into 1 cm/½ in pieces. With a swivel peeler, remove the lemon rind in thin strips and cut into fine shreds, or, if in a hurry, grate finely. Reserve the lemon juice. Have ready the garlic, sugar, sherry, stock, lemon juice and remaining cornflour blended to a paste with water.

4 Heat the oil in a wok or large frying pan and cook the chicken very quickly in small batches for 3–4 minutes until lightly coloured. Remove and keep warm while frying the rest of the chicken.

5 Add the spring onions and garlic to the pan and cook for 2 minutes.

6 Add the remaining ingredients and bring to the boil, stirring until thickened. Add more sherry or stock if necessary and stir until the chicken is evenly covered with sauce. Reheat for 2 more minutes. Serve immediately.

Sweet and Sour Kebabs

This marinade contains sugar and will burn very easily, so grill the kebabs slowly, turning often. Serve with Harlequin Rice.

Serves 4

INGREDIENTS
2 boned and skinned chicken breasts
8 pickling onions or 2 medium onions, peeled
4 rindless streaky bacon rashers
3 firm bananas
1 red pepper, seeded and diced

FOR THE MARINADE
30 ml/2 tbsp soft brown sugar
15 ml/1 tbsp Worcestershire sauce
30 ml/2 tbsp lemon juice
salt and freshly ground black pepper

FOR THE HARLEQUIN RICE
30 ml/2 tbsp olive oil
225 g/8 oz/generous 1 cup cooked rice
115 g/4 oz/1 cup cooked peas
1 small red pepper, seeded and diced

pepper

Worcestershire sauce

lemon

bacon

sugar

onions

bananas

chicken breast

1 Mix together the marinade ingredients. Cut each chicken breast into four pieces, add to the marinade, cover and leave for at least four hours or preferably overnight.

2 Peel the pickling onions, blanch them in boiling water for 5 minutes and drain. If using medium onions, quarter them after blanching.

3 Cut each rasher of bacon in half. Peel the bananas and cut each into three pieces. Wrap a rasher of bacon around each piece of banana.

4 Thread onto metal skewers with the chicken pieces, onions and pepper pieces. Brush with the marinade.

5 Grill or barbecue over low coals for 15 minutes, turning and basting frequently with the marinade. Keep warm while you prepare the rice.

COOK'S TIP
Pour boiling water over the small onions and then drain, to make peeling easier.

6 Heat the oil in a frying pan and add the rice, peas and diced pepper. Stir until heated through and serve with the kebabs.

Good

Chicken Biriani

This is a good dish for entertaining. It can be prepared in advance and reheated in the oven. Serve with traditional curry accompaniments.

Serves 8

INGREDIENTS
900 g/2 lb boneless chicken thighs
60 ml/4 tbsp olive oil
2 large onions, thinly sliced
1 – 2 green chillies, seeded and finely
   chopped
5 ml/1 tsp grated fresh root ginger
1 garlic clove, crushed
15 ml/1 tbsp hot curry powder
150 ml/¼ pint/⅔ cup chicken stock
150 ml/¼ pint/⅔ cup natural
   low fat yogurt
30 ml/2 tbsp chopped fresh coriander
salt and freshly ground black pepper

FOR THE SPICED RICE
450 g/1 lb basmati rice
2.5 ml/½ tsp garam masala
900 ml/1½ pints/3¾ cups chicken
   stock or water
50 g/2 oz/⅓ cup raisins or sultanas
25 g/1 oz/¼ cup toasted almonds

ginger

basmati rice

curry
powder

chillies

yogurt

coriander

almonds

chicken thighs

1 Put the basmati rice into a sieve and wash under cold running water to remove any starchy powder coating the grains. Then put into a bowl and cover with cold water and soak for 30 minutes. The grains will absorb some water so that they will not stick together in a solid mass while cooking.

4 Remove from the oven and then stir in the yogurt.

2 Preheat the oven to 170°C/325°F/Gas 3. Cut the chicken into cubes of approximately 2.5 cm/1 in. Heat 30 ml/2 tbsp of the oil in a large flameproof casserole, add one onion and cook until softened. Add the finely chopped chillies, ginger, garlic and curry powder and cook for a further 2 minutes, stirring occasionally.

5 Meanwhile, heat the remaining oil in a flameproof casserole and cook the remaining onion gently until tender and lightly browned. Add the drained rice, garam masala and stock or water. Bring to the boil, cover and cook in the oven with the chicken for 20–35 minutes or until tender and all the stock has been absorbed.

COOK'S TIP
Cover with buttered foil and bake in the oven for 30 minutes to reheat.

3 Add the stock and seasoning, and bring slowly to the boil. Add the chicken pieces, cover and continue cooking in the oven for 20 minutes or until tender.

6 To serve, stir the raisins or sultanas and toasted almonds into the rice. Spoon half the rice into a large deep serving dish, cover with the chicken and then the remaining rice. Sprinkle with chopped coriander to garnish.

Hot and Sour Pork

Chinese five-spice powder is made from a mixture of ground star anise, Szechuan pepper, cassia, cloves and fennel seed and has a flavour similar to liquorice. If you can't find any, use mixed spice instead.

Serves 4

INGREDIENTS

350 g/12 oz pork fillet
5 ml/1 tsp sunflower oil
2.5 cm/1 in piece root ginger, grated
1 red chilli, seeded and finely chopped
5 ml/1 tsp Chinese five-spice powder
15 ml/1 tbsp sherry vinegar
15 ml/1 tbsp soy sauce
225 g/8 oz can pineapple chunks in natural juice
175 ml/6 fl oz/¾ cup chicken stock
20 ml/4 tsp cornflour
1 small green pepper, seeded and sliced
115 g/4 oz baby sweetcorn, halved
salt and freshly ground black pepper
sprig of flat-leaf parsley, to garnish
boiled rice, to serve

pineapple chunks

pork fillet

chilli

cornflour

pepper

soy sauce

baby sweetcorn

1 Pre-heat the oven to 170°C/325°F/Gas 3. Trim away any visible fat from the pork and cut into 1 cm/½ in thick slices.

2 Brush the sunflower oil over the base of a flameproof casserole. Heat over a medium flame, then fry the meat for about 2 minutes on each side or until lightly browned.

3 Blend together the ginger, chilli, five-spice powder, vinegar and soy sauce.

4 Drain the pineapple chunks, reserving the juice. Make the stock up to 300 ml/½ pint/1¼ cups with the reserved juice, mix together with the spices and pour over the pork.

5 Slowly bring to the boil. Blend the cornflour with 15 ml/1 tbsp of cold water and gradually stir into the pork. Add the vegetables and season to taste.

6 Cover and cook in the oven for 30 minutes. Stir in the pineapple and cook for a further 5 minutes. Garnish with flat-leaf parsley and serve with boiled rice.

Honey-roast Pork with Thyme and Rosemary

Herbs and honey add flavour and sweetness to tenderloin – the leanest cut of pork.

Serves 4

INGREDIENTS
450 g/1 lb pork tenderloin
30 ml/2 tbsp thick honey
30 ml/2 tbsp Dijon mustard
5 ml/1 tsp chopped fresh rosemary
2.5 ml/½ tsp chopped fresh thyme
¼ tsp whole tropical peppercorns
sprigs of fresh rosemary and thyme, to garnish

FOR THE RED ONION CONFIT
4 red onions
350 ml/12 fl oz/1½ cups vegetable stock
15 ml/1 tbsp red wine vinegar
15 ml/1 tbsp caster sugar
1 garlic clove, crushed
30 ml/2 tbsp ruby port
pinch of salt

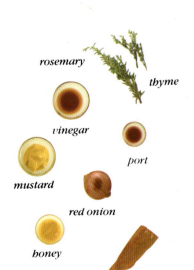

rosemary

thyme

vinegar

port

mustard

red onion

honey

pork

1 Pre-heat the oven to 180°C/350°F/Gas 4. Trim off any visible fat from the pork. Put the honey, mustard, rosemary and thyme in a small bowl and mix them together well.

2 Crush the peppercorns using a pestle and mortar. Spread the honey mixture over the pork and sprinkle with the crushed peppercorns. Place in a non-stick roasting tin and cook in the pre-heated oven for 35-45 minutes.

3 For the red onion confit, slice the onions into rings and put them into a heavy-based saucepan.

4 Add the stock, vinegar, sugar and garlic clove to the saucepan. Bring to the boil, then reduce the heat. Cover and simmer for 15 minutes.

5 Uncover and pour in the port and continue to simmer, stirring occasionally, until the onions are soft and the juices thick and syrupy. Season to taste with salt.

6 Cut the pork into slices and arrange on four warmed plates. Serve garnished with rosemary and thyme and accompanied with the red onion confit.

Fruity Lamb Tagine

The slightly sharp taste of dried fruits complements the richness of lamb in this satisfying casserole.

Serves 4

INGREDIENTS

350 g/12 oz mixed dried fruit such as apple rings, apricots, pears and prunes
675 g/1½ lb boned lean lamb
1 onion, sliced
2.5 ml/½ tsp ground ginger
5 ml/1 tsp ground coriander
large pinch of saffron strands
1 cinnamon stick
juice of 1 lemon
750 ml/1¼ pints/3⅔ cups vegetable stock
5 ml/1 tsp chopped fresh thyme
15 ml/1 tbsp clear honey
25 g/1 oz/¼ cup blanched almonds, split and toasted, to garnish
sprig of fresh thyme, to garnish
steamed cous cous, to serve

dried fruit

thyme

almonds

lamb

1 Rinse the dried fruit under cold running water. Put it into a large bowl and cover with plenty of cold water. Leave to soak for 4 hours.

2 Trim away any visible fat from the lamb and cut into 2.5 cm/1 in cubes. Add it to a large, heavy-based saucepan together with the onion, spices, lemon juice and stock. Bring to the boil, and cover with a tight fitting lid. Simmer over a low heat for 2 hours.

3 Leave to cool, then chill in the refrigerator for at least 2 hours or until the fat solidifies on the top. Skim off the fat and discard.

4 Drain the fruit and add to the lamb together with the thyme and honey. Simmer uncovered for 15 minutes. Spoon into a warmed serving dish and garnish with toasted almonds and fresh thyme. Serve with steamed cous cous.

Stir-fried Beef and Broccoli

This spicy beef may be served with noodles or on a bed of boiled rice for a speedy and low calorie Chinese meal.

Serves 4

INGREDIENTS
350 g/12 oz rump or lean prime
    casserole steak
15 ml/1 tbsp cornflour
5 ml/1 tsp sesame oil
350 g/12 oz broccoli, cut into
    small florets
4 spring onions, sliced on the diagonal
1 carrot, cut into matchstick strips
1 garlic clove, crushed
2.5 cm/1 in piece root ginger, cut into
    very fine strips
120 ml/4 fl oz/½ cup beef stock
30 ml/2 tbsp soy sauce
30 ml/2 tbsp dry sherry
10 ml/2 tsp soft light brown sugar
spring onion tassels, to garnish
noodles or rice, to serve

steak

spring
onions

ginger

broccoli

garlic

carrot

1 Trim the beef and cut into thin slices across the grain. Cut each slice into thin strips. Toss in the cornflour to coat thoroughly.

2 Heat the sesame oil in a large non-stick frying pan or wok. Add the beef strips and stir-fry over a brisk heat for 3 minutes. Remove and set aside.

COOK'S TIP

To make spring onion tassels, trim the bulb base then cut the green shoot so that the onion is 7.5 cm/3 in long. Shred to within 2.5 cm/1 in of the base and put into iced water for 1 hour.

3 Add the broccoli, spring onions, carrot, garlic clove, ginger and stock to the frying pan or wok. Cover and simmer for 3 minutes. Uncover and cook, stirring until all the stock has reduced entirely.

4 Mix the soy sauce, sherry and brown sugar together. Add to the frying pan or wok with the beef. Cook for 2–3 minutes stirring continuously. Spoon into a warm serving dish and garnish with spring onion tassels. Serve on a bed of noodles or rice.

Burgundy Steak and Mushroom Pie

Tender chunks of beef are cooked in a rich wine sauce and a crisp filo pastry crust. It won't pile on the calories, although it may taste that way.

Serves 4

INGREDIENTS
1 onion, finely chopped
175 ml/6 fl oz/¾ cup beef stock
450 g/1 lb lean chuck steak, cut into
    2.5 cm/1 in cubes
120 ml/4 fl oz/½ cup dry red wine
45 ml/3 tbsp plain flour
225 g/8 oz button mushrooms, halved
75 g/3 oz/5 sheets filo pastry
10 ml/2 tsp sunflower oil
salt and freshly ground black pepper
mashed potatoes and runner beans,
    to serve

chuck steak

onion

wine

flour

filo pastry

mushrooms

stock

1 Simmer the onion with 120 ml/ 4 fl oz/½ cup of the stock in a large covered non-stick saucepan for 5 minutes. Uncover and continue to cook, stirring occasionally, until the stock has reduced entirely. Transfer to a plate and set aside until required.

2 Add the steak to the saucepan and dry-fry until the meat is lightly browned. Return the onions to the saucepan together with the remaining stock and the red wine. Cover and simmer gently for about 1½ hours, or until tender.

3 Pre-heat the oven to 190°C/375°F/ Gas 5. Blend the flour with 45 ml/3 tbsp of cold water, add to the saucepan and simmer, stirring all the time until the sauce has thickened.

4 Add the mushrooms and continue to cook for 3 minutes. Season to taste and spoon into a 1.2 litre/2 pint/5 cup pie dish.

5 Brush a sheet of filo pastry with a little of the oil, then crumple it up loosely and place oil-side up over the filling. Repeat with the remaining pastry and oil.

6 Bake in the oven for 25-30 minutes, until the pastry is golden brown and crispy. Serve with mashed potatoes and runner beans.

Cornfed Chicken Salad

A light first course for eight people or a substantial main course for four. Arrange attractively on individual plates to serve.

Serves 8

INGREDIENTS
1 × 1.75 kg/3½ lb cornfed chicken
300 ml/½ pint/1¼ cups white wine and water, mixed
24 × 5 mm/¼ in slices French bread
1 garlic clove, peeled
225 g/8 oz French beans
115 g/4 oz fresh young spinach leaves
2 sticks celery, thinly sliced
2 spring onions, thinly sliced
2 sun-dried tomatoes, chopped
fresh chives and parsley, to garnish

FOR THE VINAIGRETTE
30 ml/2 tbsp red wine vinegar
90 ml/6 tbsp olive oil
15 ml/1 tbsp wholegrain mustard
15 ml/1 tbsp runny honey
30 ml/2 tbsp chopped mixed fresh herbs, e.g. thyme, parsley and chives
10 ml/2 tsp finely chopped capers
salt and freshly ground black pepper

honey

olive oil

cornfed chicken

spinach

red wine vinegar

French beans

1 Preheat the oven to 190°C/375°F/ Gas 5. Put the chicken into a casserole with the wine and water. Roast for 1½ hours until tender. Leave to cool in the liquid. Remove the skin and bones and cut the flesh into small pieces.

2 To make the vinaigrette, put all the ingredients into a screw-topped jar and shake vigorously to emulsify. Adjust the seasoning to taste.

3 Toast the French bread under the grill or in the oven until dry and golden brown, then lightly rub with the peeled garlic clove.

4 Trim the French beans, cut into 5 cm/ 2 in lengths and cook in boiling water until just tender (al dente). Drain and rinse under cold running water.

5 Wash the spinach, remove the stalks and tear into small pieces. Arrange on serving plates with the sliced celery, French beans, sun-dried tomatoes, chicken and spring onions.

6 Spoon over the vinaigrette dressing. Arrange the toasted croûtes on top, garnish with extra fresh chives and parsley, if desired, and serve immediately.

Dijon Chicken Salad

An attractive and elegant dish to serve for lunch with herb and garlic bread.

Serves 4

INGREDIENTS
4 boned and skinned chicken breasts
mixed salad leaves, e.g. frisée and
    oakleaf lettuce or radicchio,
    to serve

FOR THE MARINADE
30 ml/2 tbsp Dijon mustard
3 garlic cloves, crushed
15 ml/1 tbsp grated onion
60 ml/4 tbsp white wine

FOR THE MUSTARD DRESSING
30 ml/2 tbsp tarragon wine vinegar
5 ml/1 tsp Dijon mustard
5 ml/1 tsp clear honey
90 ml/6 tbsp olive oil
salt and freshly ground black pepper

white wine

honey

wine vinegar

Dijon mustard

garlic

olive oil

onion

salad leaves

chicken breasts

1 Mix all the marinade ingredients together in a shallow glass or earthenware dish that is large enough to hold the chicken in a single layer.

2 Turn the chicken over in the marinade to coat completely, cover with clear film and then chill in the refrigerator overnight.

3 Preheat the oven to 190°C/375°F/Gas 5. Transfer the chicken and the marinade into an ovenproof dish, cover with foil and bake for about 35 minutes or until tender. Leave to cool in the liquid.

4 Put all the mustard dressing ingredients into a screw-topped jar, shake vigorously to emulsify, and adjust the seasoning. (This can be made several days in advance and stored in the refrigerator.)

5 Slice the chicken thinly, fan out the slices and arrange on a serving dish with the salad leaves.

6 Spoon over some of the mustard dressing and serve.

Maryland Salad

Barbecue-grilled chicken, sweetcorn, bacon, banana and watercress combine here in a sensational main-course salad. Serve with jacket potatoes and a knob of butter.

Serves 4

INGREDIENTS
4 boneless free-range chicken breasts
salt and pepper
225 g/8 oz rindless unsmoked bacon
4 sweetcorn cobs
45 ml/3 tbsp soft butter
4 ripe bananas, peeled and halved
4 firm tomatoes, halved
1 escarole or butterhead lettuce
1 bunch watercress

DRESSING
75 ml/5 tbsp groundnut oil
15 ml/1 tbsp white wine vinegar
10 ml/2 tsp maple syrup
10 ml/2 tsp mild mustard

1 Season the chicken breasts, brush with oil and barbecue or grill for 15 minutes, turning once. Barbecue or grill the bacon for 8–10 minutes or until crisp.

2 Bring a large saucepan of salted water to the boil. Shuck and trim the corn cobs or leave the husks on if you prefer. Boil for 20 minutes. For extra flavour, brush with butter and brown over the barbecue or under the grill. Barbecue or grill the bananas and tomatoes for 6–8 minutes: you can brush these with butter too if you wish.

3 To make the dressing, combine the oil, vinegar, maple syrup and mustard with 15 ml/1 tbsp water in a screw-top jar and shake well.

sweetcorn

bananas

watercress

chicken breast

bacon

tomatoes

4 Wash, spin thoroughly and dress the salad leaves.

5 Distribute the salad leaves between 4 large plates. Slice the chicken and arrange over the leaves with the bacon, banana, sweetcorn and tomatoes.

Warm Stir-fried Salad

Warm salads are becoming increasingly popular because they are delicious and nutritious. Arrange the salad leaves on four individual plates, so the hot stir-fry can be served quickly on to them, ensuring the lettuce remains crisp and the chicken warm.

Serves 4

INGREDIENTS

15 ml/1 tbsp fresh tarragon
2 boneless, skinless chicken breasts, about 225 g/8 oz each
5 cm/2 in piece root ginger, peeled and finely chopped
45 ml/3 tbsp light soy sauce
15 ml/1 tbsp sugar
15 ml/1 tbsp sunflower oil
1 Chinese lettuce
½ frisée lettuce, torn into bite-size pieces
115 g/4 oz/1 cup unsalted cashews
2 large carrots, peeled and cut into fine strips
salt and freshly ground black pepper

chicken breast

carrot

ginger

cashews

1 Chop the tarragon.

2 Cut the chicken into fine strips and place in a bowl.

3 To make the marinade, mix together in a bowl the tarragon, ginger, soy sauce, sugar and seasoning.

4 Pour the marinade over the chicken strips and leave for 2–4 hours.

5 Strain the chicken from the marinade. Heat the wok, then add the oil. When the oil is hot, stir-fry the chicken for 3 minutes, add the marinade and bubble for 2–3 minutes.

6 Slice the Chinese lettuce and arrange on a plate with the frisée. Toss the cashews and carrots together with the chicken, pile on top of the bed of lettuce and serve immediately.

Sweet Potato Roulade

Sweet potato works particularly well as the base for this roulade. Serve in thin slices for a truly impressive dinner party dish.

Serves 6

INGREDIENTS
225 g/8 oz/1 cup low fat soft cheese such as Quark
75 ml/5 tbsp low fat yogurt
6–8 spring onions, finely sliced
30 ml/2 tbsp chopped brazil nuts, roasted
450 g/1 lb sweet potatoes, peeled and cubed
12 allspice berries, crushed
4 eggs, separated
50 g/2 oz/¼ cup Edam cheese, finely grated
salt and freshly ground black pepper
15 ml/1 tbsp sesame seeds

soft cheese

sesame seeds

sweet potato

yogurt

Edam

brazil nuts

spring onions

peppercorns

egg

1 Preheat the oven to 200°C/400°F/ Gas 6. Grease and line a 33 × 25 cm/ 13 × 10 in Swiss roll tin with non-stick baking paper, snipping the corners with scissors to fit.

2 In a small bowl, mix together the soft cheese, yogurt, spring onions and brazil nuts. Set aside.

3 Boil or steam the sweet potato until tender. Drain well. Place in a food processor with the allspice and blend until smooth. Spoon into a bowl and stir in the egg yolks and Edam. Season to taste.

4 Whisk the egg whites until stiff but not dry. Fold ⅓ of the egg whites into the sweet potatoes to lighten the mixture before gently folding in the rest.

5 Pour into the prepared tin, tipping it to get the mixture right into the corners. Smooth gently with a palette knife and cook in the oven for 10–15 minutes.

COOK'S TIP

Choose the orange-fleshed variety of sweet potato for the most striking colour.

6 Meanwhile, lay a large sheet of greaseproof paper on a clean tea-towel and sprinkle with the sesame seeds. When the roulade is cooked, tip it onto the paper, trim the edges and roll it up. Leave to cool. When cool carefully unroll, spread with the filling and roll up again. Cut into slices to serve.

Ratatouille Pancakes

These pancakes are made slightly thicker than usual to hold the juicy vegetable filling.

Serves 4

INGREDIENTS
75 g/3 oz/¾ cup plain flour
25 g/1 oz/¼ cup medium oatmeal
1 egg
300 ml/½ pint/1¼ cups
   skimmed milk
mixed salad, to serve

FOR THE FILLING
1 large aubergine, cut into 2.5 cm/1 in
   cubes
1 garlic clove, crushed
2 medium courgettes, sliced
1 green pepper, seeded and sliced
1 red pepper, seeded and sliced
75 ml/5 tbsp vegetable stock
200 g/7 oz can chopped tomatoes
5 ml/1 tsp cornflour
salt and freshly ground black pepper

1 Sift the flour and a pinch of salt into a bowl. Stir in the oatmeal. Make a well in the centre, add the egg and half the milk and mix to a smooth batter. Gradually beat in the remaining milk. Cover the bowl and leave to stand for 30 minutes.

2 Spray a 18 cm/7 in pancake pan or heavy-based frying pan with non-stick cooking spray. Heat the pan, then pour in just enough batter to cover the base of the pan thinly. Cook for 2-3 minutes, until the underside is golden brown. Flip over and cook for a further 1-2 minutes.

courgettes

oatmeal

pepper

cornflour

chopped tomatoes

aubergine

flour

egg

3 Slide the pancake out onto a plate lined with non-stick baking paper. Stack the other pancakes on top as they are made, interleaving each with non-stick baking paper. Keep warm.

4 For the filling, put the aubergine in a colander and sprinkle well with salt. Leave to stand on a plate for 30 minutes. Rinse thoroughly and drain well.

5 Put the garlic clove, courgettes, peppers, stock and tomatoes into a large saucepan. Simmer uncovered and stir occasionally for 10 minutes. Add the aubergine and cook for a further 15 minutes. Blend the cornflour with 10 ml/2 tsp water and add to the saucepan. Simmer for 2 minutes. Season to taste.

6 Spoon the ratatouille mixture into the middle of each pancake. Fold each one in half, then in half again to make a cone shape. Serve hot with a mixed salad.

Tasty

Paglia e Fieno

The title of this dish translates as 'straw and hay' which refers to the yellow and green colours of the pasta when mixed together. Using fresh peas makes all the difference to this dish.

Serves 4

INGREDIENTS

50 g/2 oz/4 tbsp low fat spread
350 g/12 oz/2 cups frozen petits pois
   or 900 g/2 lb fresh peas, shelled
150 ml/5 fl oz/⅔ cup half fat cream,
450 g/1 lb fettuccine (plain and
   spinach, mixed)
50 g/2 oz/½ cup freshly grated
   Parmesan cheese, plus extra to
   serve
freshly grated nutmeg
salt and freshly ground black pepper

tagliatelle

peas

Parmesan cheese

COOK'S TIP
Sautéed mushrooms and narrow strips of cooked ham also make a good addition.

1 Melt the low fat spread in a heavy saucepan and add the peas. Sauté for 2–3 minutes, then add the cream, bring to the boil and simmer for 1 minute until slightly thickened.

2 Cook the fettuccine in plenty of boiling salted water according to the manufacturer's instructions, but for 2 minutes' less time. The pasta should still be *al dente*. Drain very well and turn into the pan with the cream and pea sauce.

3 Place on the heat and turn the pasta in the sauce to coat. Pour in the extra and pepper to taste and a little grated nutmeg. Toss until well coated and heated through. Serve immediately with extra Parmesan cheese.

Pasta Napoletana

The simple classic cooked tomato sauce with no adornments.

Serves 4

INGREDIENTS

900 g/2 lb fresh ripe red tomatoes or
   800 g/1¾ lb canned plum tomatoes
   with juice
1 medium onion, chopped
1 medium carrot, diced
1 celery stick, diced
150 ml/5 fl oz/⅔ cup dry white wine
   (optional)
1 sprig fresh parsley
salt and pepper
pinch of caster sugar
15 ml/1 tbsp chopped fresh oregano
   or 5 ml/1 tsp dried oregano
450 g/1 lb/4 cups pasta, any variety
freshly grated Parmesan cheese, to
   serve

pasta

onion

tomatoes

celery

parsley

carrot

Parmesan cheese

1 Roughly chop the tomatoes and place in a medium saucepan.

2 Put all the ingredients except the oregano, pasta and cheese into the pan containing the tomatoes, bring to the boil and simmer, half-covered, for 45 minutes until very thick, stirring occasionally. Pass through a sieve or liquidize and sieve to remove the tomato seeds, then stir in the oregano. Taste to check the seasoning.

3 Cook the pasta in plenty of boiling salted water according to the manufacturer's instructions until *al dente*. Drain well.

4 Toss the pasta with the sauce. Serve with grated Parmesan cheese.

Spanish Omelette

Spanish omelette belongs in every cook's repertoire and can vary according to what you have in store. This version includes soft white beans and is finished with a layer of toasted sesame seeds.

VARIATION

You can also use sliced cooked potatoes, any seasonal vegetables, baby artichoke hearts and chick peas in a Spanish omelette.

Serves 4

celery

red pepper

white beans

sesame oil

sesame seeds

eggs

1 Heat the olive and sesame oils in a 30 cm/12 in paella or frying pan. Add the onion, pepper and celery and cook to soften without colouring.

2 Add the beans and continue to cook for several minutes to heat through.

3 In a small bowl beat the eggs with a fork, season well and pour over the ingredients in the pan.

4 Stir the egg mixture with a flat wooden spoon until it begins to stiffen, then allow to firm over a low heat for about 6–8 minutes.

5 Preheat a moderate grill. Sprinkle the omelette with sesame seeds and brown evenly under the grill.

6 Cut the omelette into thick wedges and serve warm with a green salad.

Carrot Mousse with Mushroom Sauce

The combination of fresh vegetables in this impressive yet easy-to-make mousse makes healthy eating a pleasure.

Serves 4

INGREDIENTS

350 g/12 oz carrots, roughly chopped
1 small red pepper, seeded and
　roughly chopped
45 ml/3 tbsp vegetable stock or water
2 eggs
1 egg white
115 g/4 oz/½ cup Quark or low fat
　soft cheese
15 ml/1 tbsp chopped fresh tarragon
salt and freshly ground black pepper
sprig of fresh tarragon, to garnish
boiled rice and leeks, to serve

FOR THE MUSHROOM SAUCE

25 g/1 oz/2 tbsp low fat spread
175 g/6 oz mushrooms, sliced
30 ml/2 tbsp plain flour
250 ml/8 fl oz/1 cup skimmed milk

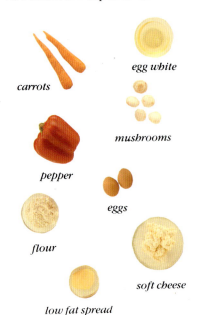

carrots

egg white

pepper

mushrooms

eggs

flour

soft cheese

low fat spread

1 Pre-heat the oven to 190°C/375°F/ Gas 5. Line the bases of four 150 ml/ ¼ pint/⅔ cup dariole moulds or ramekin dishes with non-stick baking paper. Put the carrots and red pepper in a small saucepan with the vegetable stock or water. Cover and cook for 5 minutes, or until tender. Drain well.

2 Lightly beat the eggs and egg white together. Mix the Quark or low fat soft cheese. Season to taste. Purée the cooked vegetables in a food processor or blender. Add the cheese mixture and process for a few seconds more until smooth. Stir in the chopped tarragon.

3 Divide the carrot mixture between the prepared dariole moulds or ramekin dishes and cover with foil. Place the dishes in a roasting tin half-filled with hot water. Bake in the pre-heated oven for 35 minutes, or until set.

4 For the mushroom sauce, melt 15 g/½ oz/1 tbsp of the low fat spread in a frying pan. Add the mushrooms and gently sauté for 5 minutes, until soft.

5 Put the remaining low fat spread in a small saucepan together with the flour and milk. Cook over a medium heat, stirring all the time, until the sauce thickens. Stir in the mushrooms and season to taste.

6 Turn out each mousse onto a serving plate. Spoon over a little sauce and serve the remainder separately. Garnish with a sprig of fresh tarragon and serve with boiled rice and leeks.

Tagliatelle with Walnut Sauce

An unusual sauce which would make this a spectacular dinner party starter.

Serves 4–6

INGREDIENTS
2 thick slices wholemeal bread
300 ml/10 fl oz/1¼ cups milk
275 g/10 oz/2½ cups walnut pieces
1 garlic clove, crushed
50 g/2 oz/½ cup freshly grated
   Parmesan cheese
90 ml/6 tbsp olive oil, plus extra for
   tossing the pasta
salt and pepper
450 g/1 lb tagliatelle
30 ml/2 tbsp chopped fresh parsley

1 Cut the crusts off the bread and soak in the milk until the milk is all absorbed.

2 Pre-heat the oven to 190°C/375°F/gas mark 5. Spread the walnuts on a baking sheet and toast in the oven for 5 minutes. Leave to cool.

3 Place the bread, walnuts, garlic, Parmesan cheese and olive oil in a food processor and blend until smooth. Season to taste with salt and pepper.

tagliatelle

parsley

garlic

walnut pieces

VARIATION

Add 100 g/4 oz/¾ cup stoned black olives to the food processor with the other ingredients for a richer, more piquant sauce. The Greek-style olives have the most flavour.

4 Cook the pasta in plenty of boiling salted water, drain and toss with a little olive oil. Divide the pasta equally between 4 bowls and place a dollop of sauce on each portion. Sprinkle with parsley.

Stir-fried Vegetables with Pasta

This is a colourful Chinese-style dish, easily prepared using pasta instead of Chinese noodles.

Serves 4

INGREDIENTS

1 medium carrot
175 g/6 oz small courgettes
175 g/6 oz runner or other green
   beans
175 g/6 oz baby sweetcorn
450 g/1 lb ribbon pasta such as
   tagliatelle
salt
30 ml/2 tbsp corn oil, plus extra for
   tossing the pasta
1 cm/½ in piece fresh root ginger,
   peeled and finely chopped
2 garlic cloves, finely chopped
90 ml/6 tbsp yellow bean sauce
6 spring onions sliced into
   2.5 cm/1 in lengths
30 ml/2 tbsp dry sherry
5 ml/1 tsp sesame seeds

green beans

tagliatelle

baby sweetcorn

root ginger

spring onions

courgettes

garlic

1 Slice the carrot and courgettes diagonally into chunks. Slice the beans diagonally. Cut the baby corn diagonally in half.

2 Cook the pasta in plenty of boiling salted water according to the manufacturer's instructions, drain, then rinse under hot water. Toss in a little oil.

3 Heat 30 ml/2 tbsp oil until smoking in a wok or frying pan and add the ginger and garlic. Stir-fry for 30 seconds, then add the carrots, beans and courgettes.

4 Stir-fry for 3–4 minutes, then stir in the yellow bean sauce. Stir-fry for 2 minutes, add the spring onions sherry and pasta and stir-fry for a further 1 minute until piping hot. Sprinkle with sesame seeds and serve immediately.

Pasta Tossed with Grilled Vegetables

A hearty dish to be eaten with crusty bread and washed down with a robust red wine. Try barbecuing the vegetables for a really smoky flavour.

Serves 4

INGREDIENTS
1 medium aubergine
2 medium courgettes
1 medium red pepper
8 garlic cloves, unpeeled
about 150 ml/5 fl oz/⅔ cup good olive oil
salt and pepper
450 g/1 lb ribbon pasta (pappardelle)
few sprigs fresh thyme, to garnish

olive oil

courgettes

aubergine

ribbon pasta

thyme

garlic

pepper

1 Pre-heat the grill Slice the aubergine and courgettes lengthways.

2 Halve the pepper, cut out the stalk and white pith and scrape out the seeds. Slice the pepper lengthways into 8 pieces.

3 Line a grill pan with foil and arrange the vegetables and unpeeled garlic in a single layer over the foil. Brush liberally with oil and season with salt and pepper.

4 Grill until slightly charred, turning once. If necessary, cook the vegetables in 2 batches.

5 Cool the garlic, remove the charred skins and halve. Toss the vegetables with olive oil and keep warm.

6 Meanwhile cook the pasta in plenty of boiling salted water according to the manufacturer's instructions. Drain well and toss with the grilled vegetables. Serve immediately garnished with sprigs of thyme and accompanied by plenty of country bread.

Sesame Noodle Salad with Hot Peanuts

An Orient-inspired salad with crunchy vegetables and a light soy dressing. The hot peanuts make a surprisingly successful union with the cold noodles.

Serves 4

INGREDIENTS

350 g/12 oz egg noodles
2 carrots, peeled and cut into fine
    julienne strips
½ cucumber, peeled and cut into
    1 cm/½ in cubes
115 g/4 oz celeriac, peeled and cut
    into fine julienne strips
6 spring onions, finely sliced
8 canned water chestnuts, drained
    and finely sliced
175 g/6 oz beansprouts
1 small fresh green chilli, seeded and
    finely chopped
30 ml/2 tbsp sesame seeds, to serve
115 g/4 oz/1 cup peanuts, to serve

FOR THE DRESSING

15 ml/1 tbsp dark soy sauce
15 ml/1 tbsp light soy sauce
15 ml/1 tbsp runny honey
15 ml/1 tbsp rice wine or dry sherry
15 ml/1 tbsp sesame oil

1 Preheat the oven to 200°C/400°F/ Gas 6. Cook the egg noodles in boiling water, following the instructions on the side of the packet.

2 Drain the noodles, refresh in cold water, then drain again.

3 Mix the noodles with all of the prepared vegetables.

celeriac

beansprouts

green chilli

sesame seeds

spring onion

water chestnuts

cucumber

peanuts

carrot

noodles

4 Combine the dressing ingredients in a small bowl, then toss into the noodle and vegetable mixture. Divide the salad between 4 plates.

5 Place the sesame seeds and peanuts on separate baking trays and place in the oven. Take the sesame seeds out after 5 minutes and continue to cook the peanuts for a further 5 minutes until evenly browned.

6 Sprinkle the sesame seeds and peanuts evenly over each portion and serve at once.

Coriander Ravioli with Pumpkin filling

A stunning herb pasta with a superb creamy pumpkin and roast garlic filling.

Serves 4–6

INGREDIENTS
200 g/7 oz/scant 1 cup strong
   unbleached white flour
2 eggs
pinch of salt
45 ml/3 tbsp chopped fresh coriander
coriander sprigs, to garnish

FOR THE FILLING
4 garlic cloves in their skins
450 g/1 lb pumpkin, peeled and seeds
   removed
115 g/4 oz/½ cup ricotta
4 halves sun-dried tomatoes in olive
   oil, drained and finely chopped, but
   reserve 30 ml/2 tbsp of the oil
freshly ground black pepper

coriander

egg

pumpkin

garlic

flour

ricotta

sun-dried tomatoes

1 Place the flour, eggs, salt and coriander into a food processor. Pulse until combined.

2 Place the dough on a lightly floured board and knead well for 5 minutes, until smooth. Wrap in clear film and leave to rest in the fridge for 20 minutes.

3 Preheat the oven to 200°C/400°F/ Gas 6. Place the garlic cloves on a baking sheet and bake for 10 minutes until softened. Steam the pumpkin for 5–8 minutes until tender and drain well. Peel the garlic cloves and mash into the pumpkin together with the ricotta and drained sun-dried tomatoes. Season with black pepper.

4 Divide the pasta into 4 pieces and flatten slightly. Using a pasta machine, on its thinnest setting, roll out each piece. Leave the sheets of pasta on a clean tea-towel until slightly dried.

5 Using a 7.5 cm/3 in crinkle-edged round cutter, stamp out 36 rounds.

6 Top 18 of the rounds with a teaspoonful of mixture, brush the edges with water and place another round of pasta on top. Press firmly around the edges to seal. Bring a large pan of water to the boil, add the ravioli and cook for 3–4 minutes. Drain well and toss into the reserved tomato oil. Serve garnished with coriander sprigs.

Spinach and Potato Galette

Creamy layers of potato, spinach and herbs make a warming supper dish.

Serves 6

INGREDIENTS
900 g/2 lb large potatoes
450 g/1 lb fresh spinach
2 eggs
400 g/14 oz/1¾ cup low fat cream cheese
15 ml/1 tbsp grainy mustard
50 g/2 oz chopped fresh herbs (e.g. chives, parsley, chervil or sorrel)
salt and freshly ground black pepper

mustard
parsley
cream cheese
spinach
egg
potatoes
chives

chervil
sorrel

COOK'S TIP
Choose firm potatoes for this dish such as Cara, Desirée or Estima.

1 Preheat the oven to 180°C/350°F/ Gas 4. Line a deep 23 cm/9 in cake tin with non-stick baking paper. Place the potatoes in a large pan and cover with cold water. Bring to the boil and cook for 10 minutes. Drain well and allow to cool slightly before slicing thinly.

2 Wash the spinach and place in a large pan with only the water that is clinging to the leaves. Cover and cook, stirring once, until the spinach has just wilted. Drain well in a sieve and squeeze out the excess moisture. Chop finely.

3 Beat the eggs with the cream cheese and mustard then stir in the chopped spinach and fresh herbs.

4 Place a layer of the sliced potatoes in the lined tin, arranging them in concentric circles. Top with a spoonful of the cream cheese mixture and spread out. Continue layering, seasoning with salt and pepper as you go, until all the potatoes and the cream cheese mixture are used up.

5 Cover the tin with a piece of foil and place in a roasting tin.

6 Fill the roasting tin with enough boiling water to come halfway up the sides, and cook in the oven for 45–50 minutes. Turn out onto a plate and serve hot or cold.

Spiced Vegetables with Coconut

This spicy and substantial dish could be served as a starter, or as a vegetarian main course for two. Eat it with spoons and forks, and hunks of granary bread for mopping up the delicious coconut milk.

Serves 2–4

INGREDIENTS
1 red chilli
2 large carrots
6 stalks celery
1 bulb fennel
30 ml/2 tbsp grapeseed oil
2.5 cm/1 in piece root ginger, peeled
   and grated
1 clove garlic, crushed
3 spring onions, sliced
1 × 400 ml/14 fl oz can thin
   coconut milk
15 ml/1 tbsp fresh coriander, chopped
salt and freshly ground black pepper
coriander sprigs, to garnish

celery

spring
onions

fennel

carrot

1 Halve, seed and finely chop the chilli. If necessary, wear rubber gloves to protect your hands.

2 Slice the carrots on the diagonal. Slice the celery stalks on the diagonal.

3 Trim the fennel head and slice roughly, using a sharp knife.

4 Heat the wok, then add the oil. When the oil is hot, add the ginger and garlic, chilli, carrots, celery, fennel and spring onions and stir-fry for 2 minutes.

5 Stir in the coconut milk with a large spoon and bring to the boil.

6 Stir in the coriander and salt and pepper, and serve garnished with coriander sprigs.

Mixed Roasted Vegetables

Frying Parmesan cheese in this unusual way gives
a wonderful crusty coating to the vegetables and
creates a truly Mediterranean flavour.

Serves 2

INGREDIENTS
1 large aubergine, about 225 g/8 oz
salt, for sprinkling
175 g/6 oz plum tomatoes
2 red peppers
1 yellow pepper
30 ml/2 tbsp olive oil
25 g/1 oz Parmesan cheese
30 ml/2 tbsp fresh parsley, chopped
freshly ground black pepper

peppers

plum tomatoes

aubergine

1 Cut the aubergine into segments length. Place in a colander and sprinkle with salt. Leave for 30 minutes, to allow the salt to draw out the bitter juices.

2 Rinse off the salt under cold water and pat dry on kitchen towels.

3 Cut the plum tomatoes into segments length.

4 Cut the red and yellow peppers into quarters length and seed.

5 Heat the wok, then add 5 ml/1 tsp of the olive oil. When the oil is hot, add the Parmesan and stir-fry until golden brown. Remove from the wok, allow to cool and chop into fine flakes.

6 Heat the wok, and then add the remaining oil. When the oil is hot stir-fry the aubergine and peppers for 4–5 minutes. Stir in the tomatoes and stir-fry for a further 1 minute. Toss the vegetables in the Parmesan, parsley and black pepper and serve.

Baked Squash

A creamy, sweet and nutty filling makes the perfect topping for tender buttery squash.

Serves 4

INGREDIENTS

2 butternut or acorn squash, 500 g/
   1¼ lb each
15 ml/1 tbsp olive oil
175 g/6 oz/¾ cup canned sweetcorn
   kernels, drained
115 g/4 oz/½ cup unsweetened
   chestnut purée
75 ml/5 tbsp low fat yogurt
salt and freshly ground black pepper
50 g/2 oz/¼ cup fresh goat's cheese
snipped chives, to garnish

yogurt

chestnut purée

sweetcorn

butternut squash

goat's cheese

1 Preheat the oven to 180°C/350°F/ Gas 4. Cut the squash in half length

2 Scoop out the seeds with a spoon and discard.

3 Place the squash halves on a baking sheet and brush the flesh lightly with the oil. Bake in the oven for 30 minutes.

4 Mix together the sweetcorn, chestnut purée and yogurt in a bowl. Season to taste.

5 Remove the squash from the oven and divide the chestnut mixture between them, spooning it into the hollows.

COOK'S TIP

Use mozzarella or other mild, soft cheeses in place of goat's cheese. The cheese can be omitted entirely for a lower fat alternative.

6 Top each half with ¼ of the goat's cheese and return to the oven for a further 10–15 minutes. Garnish with snipped chives.

Courgettes and Asparagus en Papillote

An impressive dinner party accompaniment, these puffed paper parcels should be broken open at the table by each guest, so that the wonderful aroma can be fully appreciated.

Serves 4

INGREDIENTS
2 medium courgettes
1 medium leek
225 g/8 oz young asparagus, trimmed
4 tarragon sprigs
4 whole garlic cloves, unpeeled
salt and freshly ground black pepper
1 egg, beaten

courgettes

asparagus

leek

egg

tarragon

garlic

1 Preheat the oven to 200°C/400°F/ Gas 6. Using a potato peeler slice the courgettes length into thin strips.

2 Cut the leek into very fine julienne strips and cut the asparagus evenly into 5 cm/2 in lengths.

3 Cut out 4 sheets of greaseproof paper measuring 30 × 38 cm/12 × 15 in and fold in half. Draw a large curve to make a heart shape when unfolded. Cut along the inside of the line and open out.

4 Divide the courgettes, asparagus and leek evenly between each paper heart, positioning the filling on one side of the fold line, and topping each with a sprig of tarragon and an unpeeled garlic clove. Season to taste.

COOK'S TIP

Experiment with other vegetables and herbs such as sugar-snap peas and mint or baby carrots and rosemary. The possibilities are endless.

5 Brush the edges lightly with the beaten egg and fold over.

6 Pleat the edges together so that each parcel is completely sealed. Lay the parcels on a baking tray and cook for 10 minutes. Serve immediately.

Broccoli and Chestnut Terrine

Served hot or cold, this versatile terrine is equally suitable for a dinner party as for a picnic.

Serves 4–6

INGREDIENTS

450 g/1 lb broccoli, cut into small florets
225 g/8 oz cooked chestnuts, roughly chopped
50 g/2 oz/1 cup fresh wholemeal breadcrumbs
60 ml/4 tbsp low fat natural yogurt
30 ml/2 tbsp Parmesan cheese, finely grated
salt, grated nutmeg and freshly ground black pepper
2 eggs, beaten

yogurt

breadcrumbs

broccoli

chestnuts

egg

Parmesan

1 Preheat the oven to 180°C/350°F/Gas 4. Line a 900 g/2 lb loaf tin with non-stick baking paper.

2 Blanch or steam the broccoli for 3–4 minutes until just tender. Drain well. Reserve ¼ of the smallest florets and chop the rest finely.

3 Mix together the chestnuts, breadcrumbs, yogurt and Parmesan, and season to taste.

4 Fold in the chopped broccoli, reserved florets and the beaten eggs.

5 Spoon the broccoli mixture into the prepared tin.

6 Place in a roasting tin and pour in boiling water to come halfway up the sides of the loaf tin. Bake for 20–25 minutes. Remove from the oven and tip out onto a plate or tray. Serve cut into even slices.

Gado Gado

Gado Gado is a traditional Indonesian salad around which friends and family gather to eat. Fillings are chosen and wrapped in a lettuce leaf. The parcel is then dipped in a spicy peanut sauce and eaten, usually with the left hand. Salad ingredients vary according to what is in season.

Serves 4

INGREDIENTS
2 medium potatoes, peeled
salt
3 eggs
175 g/6 oz green beans, topped and tailed
1 Cos lettuce
4 tomatoes, cut into wedges
115 g/4 oz bean sprouts
½ cucumber, peeled and cut into fingers
150 g/5 oz giant mooli, peeled and grated
175 g/6 oz bean curd, cut into large dice
350 g/12 oz large cooked peeled prawns
1 small bunch fresh coriander

SPICY PEANUT SAUCE
150 g/5 oz/½ cup smooth peanut butter
juice of ½ lemon
2 shallots or 1 small onion, finely chopped
1 clove garlic, crushed
1–2 small fresh red chillies, seeded and finely chopped
30 ml/2 tbsp South-east Asian fish sauce (optional)
150 ml/5 fl oz/⅔ cup coconut milk, canned or fresh
15 ml/1 tbsp caster sugar

1 To make the Spicy Peanut Sauce, combine the ingredients in a food processor until smooth.

coriander
potatoes
prawns
Cos lettuce
cucumber
eggs
green beans
bean sprouts
mooli

2 Bring the potatoes to the boil in salted water and simmer for 20 minutes. Bring a second pan of salted water to the boil. To save using too many pans, cook the eggs and beans together: lower the eggs into the boiling water in the second pan; then, after 6 minutes, add the beans and boil for a further 6 minutes. (Hard-boiled eggs should have a total of 12 minutes.) Cool the potatoes, eggs and beans under running water.

3 Wash and spin the salad leaves and use the outer leaves to line a large platter. Pile the remainder to one side of the platter.

4 Slice the potatoes. Shell and quarter the eggs. Arrange the potatoes, eggs, beans and tomatoes in separate piles. Arrange the other salad ingredients in a similar way to cover the platter.

HANDLING CHILLIES

Red chillies are considered to be sweeter and hotter than green ones. Smaller varieties of both red and green are likely to be more pungent than large varieties. You can lessen the intensity of a fresh chilli by splitting it open and removing the white seed-bearing membrane. The residue given off when chillies are cut can cause serious burns to the skin. Be sure to wash your hands thoroughly after handling raw chillies and avoid touching your eyes or any sensitive skin areas.

5 Turn the Spicy Peanut Sauce into an attractive bowl and bring to the table with the salad.

ACCOMPANIMENTS

Caponata

Caponata is a quintessential part of Sicilian antipasti and is a rich, spicy mixture of aubergine, tomatoes, capers and celery.

Serves 4

INGREDIENTS
60 ml/4 tbsp olive oil
1 large onion, sliced
2 celery sticks, sliced
450 g/1 lb aubergines, diced
5 ripe tomatoes, chopped
1 garlic clove, crushed
45 ml/3 tbsp red wine vinegar
15 ml/1 tbsp sugar
30 ml/2 tbsp capers
12 olives
pinch of salt
60 ml/4 tbsp chopped fresh parsley,
   to garnish
warm crusty bread, to serve
olives, to serve

celery

aubergines

onion   tomatoes

olives

capers

1 Heat half the oil in a large heavy saucepan. Add the onion and celery and cook over a gentle heat for about 3–4 minutes to soften.

2 Add the remainder of the oil with the aubergines and stir to absorb the oil. Cook until the aubergines begin to colour, then add the chopped tomatoes, garlic, vinegar and sugar.

3 Cover the surface of the vegetables with a circle of greaseproof paper and simmer for 8–10 minutes.

4 Add the capers and olives, then season to taste with salt. Turn the caponata out into a bowl, garnish with parsley and serve at room temperature with warm crusty bread and olives.

Crispy Cabbage

This makes a wonderful accompaniment to meat or vegetable dishes – just a couple of spoonfuls will add crispy texture to a meal. It goes especially well with prawn dishes.

Serves 2–4

INGREDIENTS
4 juniper berries
1 large Savoy cabbage
60 ml/4 tbsp vegetable oil
1 clove garlic, crushed
5 ml/1 tsp caster sugar
5 ml/1 tsp salt

cabbage

vegetable oil

garlic

juniper berries

1 Finely crush the juniper berries, using a pestle and mortar.

2 Finely shred the cabbage.

3 Heat the wok, then add the oil. When the oil is hot, stir-fry the garlic for 1 minute. Add the cabbage and stir-fry for 3–4 minutes until crispy. Remove and pat dry with kitchen towels.

4 Return the cabbage to the wok. Toss the cabbage in sugar, salt and crushed juniper berries and serve hot or cold.

Marinated Mixed Vegetables with Basil Oil

Basil oil is a must for drizzling over plain stir-fried vegetables. Once it has been made up, it will keep in the fridge for up to 2 weeks.

Serves 2–4

INGREDIENTS
15 ml/1 tbsp olive oil
1 clove garlic, crushed
rind of 1 lemon, finely grated
1 × 400 g/14 oz can artichoke hearts, drained
2 large leeks, sliced
225 g/8 oz patty pan squash, halved if large
115 g/4 oz plum tomatoes, cut into segments length
15 g/½ oz basil leaves
150 ml/¼ pint/⅔ cup olive oil
salt and freshly ground black pepper

patty pan squash

artichoke hearts

leek

plum tomatoes

2 Place the artichokes, leeks, patty pan squash and plum tomatoes in a large bowl, pour over the marinade and leave for 30 minutes.

3 Meanwhile, make the basil oil. Blend the basil leaves with the extra-virgin olive oil in a food processor until puréed.

4 Heat the wok, then stir-fry the marinated vegetables for 3–4 minutes, tossing well. Drizzle the basil oil over the vegetables and serve.

Red Cabbage in Port and Red Wine

A sweet and sour, spicy red cabbage dish, with the added crunch of pears and walnuts.

Serves 6

INGREDIENTS
15 ml/1 tbsp walnut oil
1 onion, sliced
2 whole star anise
5 ml/1 tsp ground cinnamon
pinch of ground cloves
450 g/1 lb red cabbage, finely
    shredded
25 g/1 oz/2 tbsp dark brown sugar
45 ml/3 tbsp red wine vinegar
300 ml/½ pint/1¼ cups red wine
150 ml/¼ pint/⅔ cup port
2 pears, cut into 1 cm/½ in cubes
115 g/4 oz/½ cup raisins
salt and freshly ground black pepper
115 g/4 oz/½ cup walnut halves

brown sugar

red cabbage

pears

onion   *raisins*

walnut halves

red wine vinegar

star anise

port

red wine

1 Heat the oil in a large pan. Add the onion and cook gently for about 5 minutes until softened.

2 Add the star anise, cinnamon, cloves and cabbage and cook for about 3 minutes more.

3 Stir in the sugar, vinegar, red wine and port. Cover the pan and simmer gently for 10 minutes, stirring occasionally.

4 Stir in the cubed pears and raisins and cook for a further 10 minutes or until the cabbage is tender. Season to taste. Mix in the walnut halves and serve.

Mooli, Beetroot and Carrot Stir-fry

This is a dazzling colourful dish with a crunchy texture and fragrant taste.

Serves 4 as an accompaniment

INGREDIENTS
25 g/1 oz/¼ cup pine nuts
115 g/4 oz mooli, peeled
115 g/4 oz raw beetroot, peeled
115 g/4 oz carrots, peeled
20 ml/1½ tbsp vegetable oil
juice of 1 orange
30 ml/2 tbsp fresh coriander, chopped
salt and freshly ground black pepper

pine nuts

carrot

mooli

beetroot

1 Heat the wok, then add the pine nuts and toss until golden brown. Remove and set aside.

2 Cut the mooli, beetroot and carrots into long thin strips.

3 Heat the wok and add one-third of the oil. When the oil is hot, stir-fry the mooli, beetroot and carrots for 2–3 minutes. Remove and set aside.

4 Pour the orange juice into the wok and simmer for 2 minutes. Remove and keep warm.

5 Arrange the vegetables in bundles, and sprinkle over the coriander and salt and pepper.

6 Drizzle over the orange juice, sprinkle in the pine nuts, and serve.

Grilled Mixed Peppers with Feta and Green Salsa

Soft smoky grilled peppers make a lovely combination with the slightly tart salsa.

Serves 4

INGREDIENTS

4 medium peppers in different
  colours
45 ml/3 tbsp chopped fresh flat-leaf
  parsley
45 ml/3 tbsp chopped fresh dill
45 ml/3 tbsp chopped fresh mint
½ small red onion, finely chopped
15 ml/1 tbsp capers, coarsely chopped
50 g/2 oz/¼ cup Greek olives, stoned
1 fresh green chilli, seeded and finely
  chopped
60 g/4 tbsp pistachios, chopped
75 ml/5 tbsp extra-virgin olive oil
45 ml/3 tbsp fresh lime juice
115 g/4 oz/½ cup medium fat feta
  cheese, crumbled
25 g/1 oz gherkins, finely chopped

olives
feta cheese
green chilli
mint
pistachios
peppers
gherkins
red onion

1 Preheat the grill. Place the whole peppers on a tray and grill until charred and blistered.

2 Place the peppers in a plastic bag and leave to cool.

COOK'S TIP
Feta cheese is quite salty so if preferred, soak in cold water and drain well before using.

3 Peel, seed and cut the peppers into even strips.

4 Mix all the remaining ingredients together, and stir in the pepper strips.

Beetroot and Celeriac Gratin

Beautiful ruby-red slices of beetroot and celeriac make a stunning light accompaniment to any main course dish.

Serves 6

INGREDIENTS
350 g/12 oz raw beetroot
350 g/12 oz celeriac
4 thyme sprigs
6 juniper berries, crushed
salt and freshly ground black pepper
100 ml/4 fl oz/½ cup fresh orange
    juice
100 ml/4 fl oz/½ cup vegetable stock

celeriac

orange juice

juniper berries

beetroot

thyme

1 Preheat the oven to 190°C/375°F/ Gas 5. Peel and slice the beetroot very finely. Quarter and peel the celeriac and slice very finely.

2 Fill a 25 cm/10 in diameter, cast iron, ovenproof or flameproof frying pan with alternate layers of beetroot and celeriac slices, sprinkling with the thyme, juniper and seasoning between each layer.

3 Mix the orange juice and stock together and pour over the gratin. Place over a medium heat and bring to the boil. Boil for 2 minutes.

4 Cover with foil and place in the oven for 15–20 minutes. Remove the foil and raise the oven temperature to 200°C/ 400°F/Gas 6. Cook for a further 10 minutes.

Mixed Mushroom Ragout

These mushrooms are delicious served hot or cold and can be made up to two days in advance.

Serves 4

INGREDIENTS
1 small onion, finely chopped
1 garlic clove, crushed
5 ml/1 tsp coriander seeds, crushed
30 ml/2 tbsp red wine vinegar
15 ml/1 tbsp soy sauce
15 ml/1 tbsp dry sherry
10 ml/2 tsp tomato purée
10 ml/2 tsp soft light brown sugar
150 ml/¼ pint/⅔ cup vegetable stock
115 g/4 oz baby button mushrooms
115 g/4 oz chestnut mushrooms, quartered
115 g/4 oz oyster mushrooms, sliced
salt and freshly ground black pepper
sprig of fresh coriander, to garnish

oyster mushrooms

sherry

chestnut mushrooms

soy sauce

coriander seeds

vinegar

tomato purée

garlic

coriander

button mushrooms

onion

1 Put the first nine ingredients into a large saucepan. Bring to the boil and reduce the heat. Cover and simmer for 5 minutes.

2 Uncover the saucepan and simmer for 5 more minutes, or until the liquid has reduced by half.

3 Add the baby button and chestnut mushrooms and simmer for 3 minutes. Stir in the oyster mushrooms and cook for a further 2 minutes.

4 Remove the mushrooms with a slotted spoon and transfer them to a serving dish.

5 Boil the juices for about 5 minutes, or until reduced to about 75 ml/5 tbsp. Season to taste.

6 Allow to cool for 2-3 minutes, then pour over the mushrooms. Serve hot or well chilled, garnished with a sprig of fresh coriander.

Rocket, Pear and Parmesan Salad

For a sophisticated start to an elaborate meal, try this simple salad of honey-rich pears, fresh Parmesan and aromatic leaves of rocket. Enjoy with a young Beaujolais or chilled Lambrusco wine.

Serves 4

INGREDIENTS
3 ripe pears, Williams or Packhams
10 ml/2 tsp lemon juice
45 ml/3 tbsp hazelnut or walnut oil
125 g/4 oz rocket
75 g/3 oz Parmesan cheese
black pepper
open-textured bread, to serve

rocket

Parmesan cheese

pears

1 Peel and core the pears and slice thickly. Moisten with lemon juice to keep the flesh white.

2 Combine the nut oil with the pears. Add the rocket leaves and toss.

3 Turn the salad out on to 4 small plates and top with shavings of Parmesan cheese. Season with freshly ground black pepper and serve.

COOK'S TIP
If you are unable to buy rocket easily, you can grow your own from early spring to late summer.

Leek and Caraway Gratin with a Carrot Crust

Tender leeks are mixed with a creamy caraway sauce and a crunchy carrot topping.

Serves 4–6

INGREDIENTS

675 g/1½ lb leeks, cut into 5 cm/2 in
   pieces
150 ml/¼ pint/⅔ cup vegetable stock
   or water
45 ml/3 tbsp dry white wine
5 ml/1 tsp caraway seeds
pinch of salt
300 ml/10 fl oz/1¼ cups skimmed
   milk as required
25 g/1 oz/2 tbsp butter
25 g/1 oz/¼ cup plain flour

FOR THE TOPPING

115 g/4 oz/2 cups fresh wholemeal
   breadcrumbs
115 g/4 oz/2 cups grated carrot
30 ml/2 tbsp chopped fresh parsley
75 g/3 oz Jarlsberg cheese, coarsely
   grated
25 g/1 oz/2 tbsp slivered almonds

parsley

vegetable stock

Jarlsberg

leek

breadcrumbs

butter

1 Place the leeks in a large pan. Add the stock or water, wine, caraway seeds and salt. Bring to a simmer, cover and cook for 5–7 minutes until the leeks are just tender.

2 With a slotted spoon, transfer the leeks to an ovenproof dish. Reduce the remaining liquid to half then make the amount up to 350 ml/12 fl oz/1½ cups with skimmed milk.

3 Preheat the oven to 180°C/350°F/ Gas 4. Melt the butter in a saucepan, stir in the flour and cook without allowing it to colour for 1–2 minutes. Gradually add the stock and milk, stirring well after each addition, until you have a smooth sauce. Simmer for 5–6 minutes then pour over the leeks in the dish.

4 Mix all the topping ingredients together in a bowl and sprinkle over the leeks. Bake for 20–25 minutes until golden.

Apple Coleslaw

The term coleslaw stems from the Dutch *koolsla*, meaning 'cool cabbage'. There are many variations of this salad; this recipe combines the sweet flavours of apple and carrot with celery salt. Coleslaw is traditionally served with cold ham.

Serves 4

INGREDIENTS
450 g/1 lb white cabbage
1 medium onion
2 apples, peeled and cored
175 g/6 oz carrots, peeled
150 ml/5 fl oz/²⁄₃ cup mayonnaise
5 ml/1 tsp celery salt
black pepper

carrots

onion

apple

white cabbage

2 Feed the cabbage and the onion through a food processor fitted with a slicing blade. Change to a grating blade and grate the apples and carrots. Alternatively use a hand grater and vegetable slicer.

3 Combine the salad ingredients in a large bowl. Fold in the mayonnaise and season with celery salt and freshly ground black pepper.

1 Discard the outside leaves of the cabbage if they are dirty, cut the cabbage into 5 cm/2 in wedges, then remove the stem section.

COOK'S TIP

This recipe can be adapted easily to suit different tastes. You could add 125 g/4 oz/½ cup chopped walnuts or raisins for added texture. For a richer coleslaw, add 125 g/4 oz/½ cup grated Cheddar cheese. You may find you will need smaller portions, as the cheese makes a more filling dish.

Sweet Turnip Salad with Horseradish and Caraway

The robust-flavoured turnip partners well with the taste of horseradish and caraway seeds. This salad is delicious with cold roast beef or smoked trout.

Serves 4

INGREDIENTS
350 g/12 oz medium turnips
2 spring onions , white part
    only, chopped
15 ml/1 tbsp caster sugar
salt
30 ml/2 tbsp horseradish cream
10 ml/2 tsp caraway seeds

turnips

spring onions

COOK'S TIP

If turnips are not available, giant white radish can be used as a substitute.

1 Peel, slice and shred the turnips – or grate them if you wish.

2 Add the spring onions sugar and salt, then rub together with your hands to soften the turnip.

3 Fold in the horseradish cream and caraway seeds.

DESSERTS AND BAKING

Strawberry Conchiglie Salad with Kirsch and Raspberry Sauce

A divinely decadent dessert laced with liqueur and luscious raspberry sauce.

Serves 4

INGREDIENTS
175 g/6 oz/½ cup pasta shells
salt
225 g/8 oz fresh or frozen raspberries, thawed if frozen
15–30 ml/1–2 tbsp caster sugar
lemon juice
450 g/1 lb small fresh strawberries
flaked almonds
45 ml/3 tbsp kirsch

pasta shells

raspberries

strawberries

almonds

1 Cook the pasta in plenty of boiling salted water according to the manufacturer's instructions. Drain well and cool.

2 Purée the raspberries in a food processor and pass through a sieve (strainer) to remove the seeds.

3 Put the purée in a small saucepan with the sugar and simmer for 5–6 minutes, stirring occasionally. Add lemon juice to taste. Set aside to cool.

4 Hull the strawberries and halve if necessary. Toss with the pasta and transfer to a serving bowl.

5 Spread the almonds on a baking sheet and toast under the grill (broiler) until golden. Cool.

6 Stir the kirsch into the raspberry sauce and pour over the salad. Scatter with the toasted almonds and serve.

Apricot Delice

A fluffy mousse base with a layer of fruit jelly on top makes this dessert doubly delicious.

Serves 8

INGREDIENTS

2 × 400 g/14 oz cans apricots in natural juice
60 ml/4 tbsp fructose
15 ml/1 tbsp lemon juice
25 ml/5 tsp powdered gelatine
425 g/15 oz low fat ready-to-serve custard
150 ml/¼ pint/⅔ cup strained yogurt
yogurt piping cream to decorate
1 apricot, sliced and sprig of fresh apple mint, to decorate

canned apricots

gelatine

custard

strained yogurt

apricots

1 Line the base of a 1.2 litre/2 pint/5 cup heart-shaped or round cake tin with non-stick baking paper.

2 Drain the apricots, reserving the juice. Put the drained apricots in a food processor or blender fitted with a metal blade together with the fructose and 60 ml/4 tbsp of the apricot juice. Blend to a smooth purée.

3 Measure 30 ml/2 tbsp of the apricot juice into a small bowl. Add the lemon juice, then sprinkle over 10 ml/2 tsp of the gelatine. Leave for about 5 minutes, until 'spongy'.

4 Stir the gelatine into half of the purée and pour into the prepared tin. Chill in a refrigerator for 1½ hours, or until firm.

COOK'S TIP

Don't use a loose-bottomed cake tin for this recipe as the mixture may seep through before it sets.

5 Sprinkle the remaining 15 ml/1 tbsp of gelatine over 60 ml/4 tbsp of the apricot juice. Soak and dissolve as before. Mix the remaining apricot purée with the custard, yogurt and gelatine. Pour onto the layer of set fruit purée and chill in the refrigerator for 3 hours.

6 Dip the cake tin into hot water for a few seconds and unmould the delice onto a serving plate. Decorate with yogurt piping cream, the sliced apricot and sprigs of fresh apple mint.

Raspberry Salad with Mango Custard Sauce

This remarkable salad unites the sharp quality of fresh raspberries with a special custard made from rich fragrant mangoes.

Serves 4

INGREDIENTS
1 large mango
3 egg yolks
30 ml/2 tbsp caster sugar
10 ml/2 tsp cornflour
200 ml/7 fl oz/scant 1 cup milk
8 sprigs fresh mint

RASPBERRY SAUCE
500 g/1 lb 2 oz raspberries
45 ml/3 tbsp caster sugar

eggs

mint

mango

raspberries

COOK'S TIP

Mangoes are ripe when they yield to gentle pressure in the hand. Some varieties show a red-gold or yellow flush when they are ready to eat.

1 To prepare the mango, remove the top and bottom with a serrated knife. Cut away the outer skin, then remove the flesh by cutting either side of the flat central stone. Save one half of the fruit for decoration and roughly chop the remainder.

2 For the custard, combine the egg yolks, sugar, cornflour and 30 ml/2 tbsp of the milk smoothly in a bowl.

3 Rinse a small saucepan out with cold water to prevent the milk from catching. Bring the rest of the milk to the boil in the pan, pour it over the ingredients in the bowl and stir evenly.

4 Sieve the mixture back into the saucepan, stir to a simmer and allow the mixture to thicken.

5 Pour the custard into a food processor, add the chopped mango and blend until smooth. Allow to cool.

6 To make the raspberry sauce, place 350 g/12 oz of the raspberries in a stain-resistant saucepan. Add the sugar, soften over a gentle heat and simmer for 5 minutes. Rub the fruit through a fine nylon sieve to remove the seeds. Allow to cool.

7 Spoon the raspberry sauce and mango custard into 2 pools on 4 plates. Slice the reserved mango and fan out or arrange in a pattern over the raspberry sauce. Scatter fresh raspberries over the mango custard. Decorate with 2 sprigs of mint and serve.

Iced Pineapple Crush with Strawberries and Lychees

The sweet tropical flavours of pineapple and lychees combine well with richly scented strawberries to make this a most refreshing salad.

Serves 4

INGREDIENTS
2 small pineapples
450 g/1 lb strawberries
400 g/14 oz can lychees
45 ml/3 tbsp kirsch or white rum
30 ml/2 tbsp icing sugar

pineapple

strawberries

1 Remove the crown from both pineapples by twisting sharply. Reserve the leaves for decoration.

2 Cut the fruit in half diagonally with a large serrated knife.

3 Cut around the flesh inside the skin with a small serrated knife, keeping the skin intact. Remove the core from the pineapple.

4 Chop the pineapple and combine with the strawberries and lychees, taking care not to damage the fruit.

COOK'S TIP

A ripe pineapple will resist pressure when squeezed and will have a sweet, fragrant smell. In winter freezing conditions can cause the flesh to blacken.

5 Combine the kirsch with the icing sugar, pour over the fruit and freeze for 45 minutes.

6 Turn the fruit out into the pineapple skins and decorate with pineapple leaves.

Watermelon Sorbet

A slice of this refreshing sorbet is the perfect way to cool down on a hot sunny day.

Serves 4–6

INGREDIENTS
½ small watermelon, weighing about
   1 kg/2¼ lb
75 g/3 oz/½ cup caster sugar
60 ml/4 tbsp cranberry juice or water
30 ml/2 tbsp lemon juice
sprigs of fresh mint, to decorate

cranberry juice

sugar

watermelon   *lemon juice*

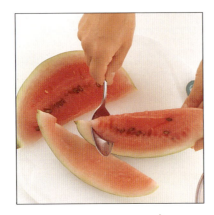

1 Cut the watermelon into 4–6 equal-sized wedges (depending on the number of servings you require). Scoop out the pink flesh, discarding the seeds but reserving the shell.

2 Line a freezer-proof bowl, about the same size as the melon, with clear film. Arrange the melon skins in the bowl to re-form the shell, fitting them together snugly so that there are no gaps. Put in the freezer.

3 Put the sugar and cranberry juice or water in a saucepan and stir over a low heat until the sugar dissolves. Bring to the boil and simmer for 5 minutes. Leave the sugar syrup to cool.

4 Put the melon flesh and lemon juice in a blender and process to a smooth purée. Stir in the sugar syrup and pour into a freezer-proof container. Freeze for 3–3½ hours, or until slushy.

5 Tip the sorbet into a chilled bowl and whisk to break up the ice crystals. Return to the freezer for another 30 minutes, whisk again, then tip into the melon shell and freeze until solid.

6 Remove from the freezer and leave to defrost at room temperature for 15 minutes. Take the melon out of the bowl and cut into wedges with a warmed sharp knife. Serve with sprigs of fresh mint.

COOK'S TIP
If preferred, this pretty pink sorbet can be served scooped into balls. Do this before the mixture is completely frozen and re-freeze the balls on a baking sheet, ready to serve.

Mango and Coconut Stir-fry

Choose a ripe mango for this recipe. If you buy one that is a little under-ripe, leave it in a warm place for a day or two before using.

Serves 4

INGREDIENTS
¼ coconut
1 large, ripe mango
juice of 2 limes
rind of 2 limes, finely grated
15 ml/1 tbsp sunflower oil
15 g/½ oz/1 tbsp butter
30 ml/1½ tbsp clear honey
crème fraîche, to serve

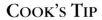 coconut

mango

honey

lime

COOK'S TIP

Because of the delicate taste of desserts, always make sure your wok has been scrupulously cleaned so there is no transference of flavours – a garlicky mango isn't quite the effect you want to achieve!

1 Prepare the coconut flakes by draining the milk from the coconut and peeling the flesh with a vegetable peeler.

2 Peel the mango. Cut the stone out of the middle of the fruit. Cut each half of the mango into slices.

3 Place the mango slices in a bowl and pour over the lime juice and rind, to marinate them.

4 Meanwhile, heat the wok, then add 10 ml/2 tsp of the oil. When the oil is hot, add the butter. When the butter has melted, stir in the coconut flakes and stir-fry for 1–2 minutes until the coconut is golden brown. Remove and drain on kitchen towels. Wipe out the wok. Strain the mango slices, reserving the juice.

5 Heat the wok and add the remaining oil. When the oil is hot, add the mango and stir-fry for 1–2 minutes, then add the juice and allow to bubble and reduce for 1 minute. Then stir in the honey, sprinkle on the coconut flakes and serve with crème fraîche.

Feather-light Peach Pudding

On chilly days, try this hot fruit pudding with its tantalizing sponge topping.

Serves 4

INGREDIENTS

400 g/14 oz can peach slices in
    natural juice
50 g/2 oz/4 tbsp low fat spread
40 g/1½ oz/¼ cup soft light
    brown sugar
1 egg, beaten
65 g/2½ oz/½ cup plain
    wholemeal flour
50 g/2 oz/½ cup plain flour
5 ml/1 tsp baking powder
2.5 ml/½ tsp ground cinnamon
60 ml/4 tbsp skimmed milk
2.5 ml/½ tsp vanilla essence
10 ml/2 tsp icing sugar, for dusting
low fat ready-to-serve custard,
    to serve

peach slices

flour

icing
sugar

egg

brown sugar

low fat
custard

1 Pre-heat the oven to 180°C/350°F/ Gas 4. Drain the peaches and put into a 1 litre/1¾ pint/4 cup pie dish with 30 ml/ 2 tbsp of the juice.

2 Put all the remaining ingredients, except the icing sugar into a mixing bowl. Beat for 3–4 minutes, until thoroughly combined.

COOK'S TIP

For a simple sauce, blend 5 ml/1 tsp arrowroot with 15 ml/1 tbsp peach juice in a small saucepan. Stir in the remaining peach juice from the can and bring to the boil. Simmer for 1 minute until thickened and clear.

3 Spoon the sponge mixture over the peaches and level the top evenly. Cook in the oven for 35-40 minutes, or until springy to the touch.

4 Lightly dust the top with icing sugar before serving hot with the custard.

Plum, Rum and Raisin Brûlée

Crack through the crunchy caramel to find the juicy plums and smooth creamy centre of this dessert.

Serves 4

INGREDIENTS
25 g/1 oz/3 tbsp raisins
15 ml/1 tbsp dark rum
350 g/12 oz medium plums (about 6)
juice of 1 orange
15 ml/1 tbsp clear honey
225 g/8 oz/2 cups low fat soft cheese
90 g/3½ oz/½ cup granulated sugar

raisins

rum

orange

plums

honey

1 Put the raisins into a small bowl and sprinkle over the rum. Leave to soak for 5 minutes.

2 Quarter the plums and remove their stones. Put into a large, heavy-based saucepan together with the orange juice and honey. Simmer gently for 5 minutes or until soft. Stir in the soaked raisins. Reserve 15 ml/1 tbsp of the juice, then divide the rest between four 150 ml/¼ pint/⅔ cup ramekin dishes.

3 Blend the low fat soft cheese with the reserved 15 ml/1 tbsp of plum juice. Spoon over the plums and chill in the refrigerator for 1 hour.

4 Put the sugar into a large, heavy-based saucepan with 45 ml/3 tbsp cold water. Heat gently, stirring, until the sugar has dissolved. Boil for 15 minutes or until it turns golden brown. Cool for 2 minutes, then carefully pour over the ramekins. Cool and serve.

Blushing Pears

Pears poached in rosé wine and sweet spices absorb
all the subtle flavours and turn a soft pink colour.

Serves 6

INGREDIENTS
6 firm eating pears
300 ml/½ pint/1¼ cups rosé wine
150 ml/¼ pint/⅔ cup cranberry or
  clear apple juice
strip of thinly pared orange rind
1 cinnamon stick
4 whole cloves
1 bay leaf
75 ml/5 tbsp caster sugar
small bay leaves, to decorate

wine

pears   *cranberry juice*

cinnamon

sugar

orange

1 Thinly peel the pears with a sharp knife or vegetable peeler, leaving the stalks attached.

2 Pour the wine and cranberry or apple juice into a large heavy-based saucepan. Add the orange rind, cinnamon stick, cloves, bay leaf and sugar.

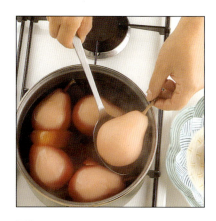

3 Heat gently, stirring all the time until the sugar has dissolved. Add the pears and stand them upright in the pan. Pour in enough cold water to barely cover them. Cover and cook very gently for 20–30 minutes, or until just tender, turning and basting occasionally.

4 Using a slotted spoon, gently lift the pears out of the syrup and transfer to a serving dish.

5 Bring the syrup to the boil and boil rapidly for 10–15 minutes, or until it has reduced by half.

COOK'S TIP
Check the pears by piercing with a skewer or sharp knife towards the end of the poaching time because some may cook more quickly than others.

6 Strain the syrup and pour over the pears. Serve hot or well-chilled, decorated with bay leaves.

Carrot and Courgette Cake

If you can't resist the lure of a slice of iced cake, you'll love this moist, spiced sponge with its delicious creamy topping.

Serves 10

INGREDIENTS
1 medium carrot
1 medium courgette
3 eggs, separated
115 g/4 oz/scant ½ cup soft light brown sugar
30 ml/2 tbsp ground almonds
finely grated rind of 1 orange
150 g/5 oz/1 cup self-raising wholemeal flour
5 ml/1 tsp ground cinnamon
5 ml/1 tsp icing sugar, to dust
fondant carrots and courgettes, to decorate

FOR THE TOPPING
175 g/6 oz/¾ cup low fat soft cheese
5 ml/1 tsp clear honey

fondant decorations

egg

cinnamon

courgette

brown sugar

carrot

orange

honey

1 Pre-heat the oven to 180°C/350°F/Gas 4. Line an 18 cm/7 in square tin with non-stick baking paper. Coarsely grate the carrot and courgette.

2 Put the egg yolks, sugar, ground almonds and orange rind into a bowl and whisk until very thick and light.

3 Sift together the flour and cinnamon and fold into the mixture together with the grated vegetables. Add any bran left over from the flour in the sieve.

4 Whisk the egg whites until stiff and carefully fold them in, a half at a time. Spoon into the prepared tin. Bake in the oven for 1 hour and cover the top with foil after 40 minutes.

5 Leave to cool in the tin for 5 minutes, then turn out onto a wire rack and carefully remove the lining paper.

6 For the topping, beat together the cheese and honey and spread over the cake. Decorate with fondant carrots and courgettes.

Cheese and Chive Scones

Feta cheese makes an excellent substitute for butter in these tangy savoury scones.

Makes 9

INGREDIENTS
115 g/4 oz/1 cup self-raising flour
150 g/5 oz/1 cup self-raising
   wholemeal flour
2.5 ml/½ tsp salt
75 g/3 oz feta cheese
15 ml/1 tbsp snipped fresh chives
150 ml/¼ pint/⅔ cup skimmed milk,
   plus extra for glazing
1.25 ml/¼ tsp cayenne pepper

flour

feta cheese

chives

cayenne pepper

wholemeal flour

milk

1 Pre-heat the oven to 200°C/400°F/ Gas 6. Sift the flours and salt into a mixing bowl, adding any bran left over from the flour in the sieve.

2 Crumble the feta cheese and rub into the dry ingredients. Stir in the chives, then add the milk and mix to a soft dough.

3 Turn out onto a floured surface and lightly knead until smooth. Roll out to 2 cm/¾ in thick and stamp out nine scones with a 6 cm/2½ in biscuit cutter.

4 Transfer the scones to a non-stick baking sheet. Brush with skimmed milk, then sprinkle over the cayenne pepper. Bake in the oven for 15 minutes, or until golden brown. Serve warm or cold.

Sage Soda Bread

This wonderful loaf, quite unlike bread made with yeast, has a velvety texture and a powerful sage aroma.

Makes 1 loaf

INGREDIENTS
225 g/8 oz/2 cups wholemeal flour
115 g/4 oz/1 cup strong white flour
2.5 ml/½ tsp salt
5 ml/1 tsp bicarbonate of soda
30 ml/2 tbsp shredded fresh sage
300−450 ml/½−¾ pint/1¼−1¾ cups buttermilk

white flour

wholemeal flour

sage

buttermilk

1 Preheat the oven to 220°C/425°F/ Gas 7. Sift the dry ingredients into a bowl.

2 Stir in the sage and add enough buttermilk to make a soft dough.

COOK'S TIP

As an alternative to the sage, try using finely chopped rosemary or thyme.

3 Shape the dough into a round loaf and place on a lightly oiled baking sheet.

4 Cut a deep cross in the top. Bake in the oven for 40 minutes until the loaf is well risen and sounds hollow when tapped on the bottom. Leave to cool on a wire rack.

Chocolate and Orange Angel Cake

This light-as-air sponge with its fluffy icing is virtually fat free, yet tastes heavenly.

Serves 10

INGREDIENTS
25 g/1 oz/¼ cup plain flour
15 g/½ oz/2 tbsp fat reduced cocoa powder
15 g/½ oz/2 tbsp cornflour
pinch of salt
5 egg whites
2.5 ml/½ tsp cream of tartar
115 g/4 oz/scant ½ cup caster sugar
blanched and shredded rind of 1 orange, to decorate

ICING
200 g/7 oz/1 cup caster sugar
1 egg white

sugar

egg

cornflour

orange

flour

cocoa

1 Preheat the oven to 180°C/350°F/Gas 4. Sift the flour, cocoa powder, cornflour and salt together three times. Beat the egg whites in a large bowl until foamy. Add the cream of tartar, then whisk until soft peaks form.

2 Add the caster sugar to the egg whites a spoonful at a time, whisking after each addition. Sift a third of the flour and cocoa mixture over the meringue and gently fold in. Repeat, sifting and folding in the flour and cocoa mixture two more times.

3 Spoon the mixture into a non-stick 20 cm/8 in ring mould and level the top. Bake in the oven for 35 minutes or until springy when lightly pressed. Turn upside-down onto a wire rack and leave to cool in the tin. Carefully ease out of the tin.

4 For the icing, put the sugar in a pan with 75 ml/5 tbsp cold water. Stir over a low heat until dissolved. Boil until the syrup reaches a temperature of 120°C/240°F on a sugar thermometer, or when a drop of the syrup makes a soft ball when dropped into a cup of cold water. Remove from the heat.

5 Whisk the egg white until stiff. Add the syrup in a thin stream, whisking all the time. Continue to whisk until the mixture is very thick and fluffy.

COOK'S TIP

Make sure you do not over-beat the egg whites. They should not be stiff but should form soft peaks, so that the air bubbles can expand further during cooking and help the cake to rise.

6 Spread the icing over the top and sides of the cooled cake. Sprinkle the orange rind over the top of the cake and serve.

Courgette and Walnut Loaf

Cardamom seeds impart their distinctive aroma to this loaf. Serve spread with ricotta and honey for a delicious snack.

Makes 1 loaf

INGREDIENTS

3 × size 3 eggs
75 g/3 oz/⅓ cup light muscovado sugar
100 ml/4 fl oz/½ cup sunflower oil
225 g/8 oz/2 cups wholemeal flour
5 ml/1 tsp baking powder
5 ml/1 tsp bicarbonate of soda
5 ml/1 tsp ground cinnamon
3 ml/¾ tsp ground allspice
7.5 ml/½ tbsp green cardamoms, seeds removed and crushed
150 g/5 oz courgette, coarsely grated
115 g/4 oz/½ cup walnuts, chopped
50 g/2 oz/¼ cup sunflower seeds

courgettes

walnuts   egg

sunflower oil

muscovado sugar

wholemeal flour

sunflower seeds

cardamom pods

1 Preheat the oven to 180°C/350°F/Gas 4. Line the base and sides of a 900 g/2 lb loaf tin with non-stick baking paper.

2 Beat the eggs and sugar together and gradually add the oil.

3 Sift the flour into a bowl together with the baking powder, bicarbonate of soda, cinnamon and allspice.

4 Mix into the egg mixture with the rest of the ingredients, reserving 15 g/1 tbsp of the sunflower seeds for the top.

5 Spoon into the loaf tin, level off the top, and sprinkle with the reserved sunflower seeds.

6 Bake for 1 hour or until a skewer inserted in the centre comes out clean. Leave to cool slightly before turning out onto a wire rack to cool completely.

Saffron Focaccia

A dazzling yellow bread that is light in texture and distinctive in flavour.

Makes 1 loaf

INGREDIENTS
pinch of saffron threads
150 ml/¼ pint/⅔ cup boiling water
225 g/8 oz/2 cups plain flour
2.5 ml/½ tsp salt
5 ml/1 tsp easy-blend dry yeast
15 ml/1 tbsp olive oil

FOR THE TOPPING
2 garlic cloves, sliced
1 red onion, cut into thin wedges
rosemary sprigs
12 black olives, stoned and coarsely
    chopped
15 ml/1 tbsp olive oil

flour

garlic

rosemary

red onion

olives

saffron

yeast

1 Place the saffron in a heatproof jug and pour on the boiling water. Leave to stand and infuse until lukewarm.

2 Place the flour, salt, yeast and olive oil in a food processor. Turn on and gradually add the saffron and its liquid. Process until the dough forms into a ball.

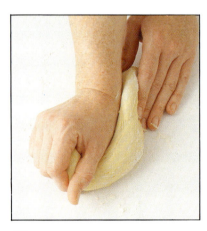

3 Turn onto a floured board and knead for 10–15 minutes. Place in a bowl, cover and leave to rise for 30–40 minutes until doubled in size.

4 Punch down the risen dough on a lightly floured surface and roll out into an oval shape, 1 cm/½ in thick. Place on a lightly greased baking tray and leave to rise for 20–30 minutes.

5 Preheat the oven to 200°C/400°F/Gas 6. Use your fingers to press small indentations all over the surface of the focaccia.

6 Cover with the topping ingredients, brush lightly with olive oil, and bake for 25 minutes or until the loaf sounds hollow when tapped on the bottom. Leave to cool on a wire rack.

INDEX

INDEX

INDEX